A Detailed Biblical Introduction To The End Times

The Pre-Tribulation Rapture, Seven-Year Tribulation, and Pre-Millennial Return of Jesus Christ

Arden Kierce

Copyright © 2023, Arden Kierce. All rights reserved.

ISBN-13: 9798387054556

Reproduction in whole or in part is prohibited without prior written permission from the publisher. This work is intended to provide general information only. The author and publisher do not accept liability for damage or injury resulting from reliance on the information within this work.

Scripture quotations labeled KJV are from the King James Version of the Bible.

A Detailed Biblical Introduction To The End Times

TABLE OF CONTENTS

Introduction 3

Chapter 1: Different Perspectives of the End Times 7

Chapter 2: The Rapture and Its Timing 25

Chapter 3: Signs of the End Times 55

Chapter 4: The Events of the Tribulation 95

Chapter 5: The Antichrist, His Empire, Babylon, and the Abomination of Desolation 138

Chapter 6: The False Prophet and the Image of the Beast 180

Chapter 7: The Mark of the Beast 188

Chapter 8: The Purpose of the Tribulation and the Second Coming of Jesus 215

Chapter 9: What The End Times Mean For You Today . . 249

Conclusion 271

Appendix: Some Remaining Questions 273

Recommended Sources For Further Study 304

Other Books By Arden Kierce 309

Arden Kierce

Introduction

Are we living in the end times? What does the Bible say will happen in the last days of this world? What are the signs that show this time is approaching, and how will the future unfold?

According to the Bible, the *end times* or *last days* of the world actually began during Jesus Christ's ministry in the early first century AD (Hebrews 1:2, 1 Peter 1:20). Some more signs of the end times were fulfilled not long after Jesus' resurrection, when the Church began (Acts 2:16–18).

However, usually, when people talk about the end times, they are referring to a specific period of approximately seven years that is described in the biblical Book of Revelation, as well as in a few other parts of the Bible. This period of seven years is often called *the Tribulation*, or sometimes *the time of Jacob's trouble* (Jeremiah 30:7, Daniel 12:1).

The term *Tribulation* comes from the word used by Jesus in some English Bible translations of Matthew

24:21 and 24:29. Here, Jesus refers to a period of time when the world will face great difficulties and divinely-appointed judgments before Jesus returns to earth at his Second Coming.

Jesus also said there will be signs that will tell people who are watching that the end times are approaching. Quite a few Christians today believe that these signs are increasing in frequency and intensity. So it is not surprising that many people are becoming more interested in studying what the Bible teaches about the end times.

However, learning about the end times can be challenging. There are many sources of information out there, and differing opinions on how to interpret the Bible on this topic.

This book aims to provide a concise and easy-to-understand introduction to what the Bible teaches about the end times. It will also provide a detailed introduction to the ideas and terminology found in discussions of Bible prophecy by expert scholars. Yet no pre-existing knowledge of the Bible or Christianity is necessary before beginning to read this introduction.

Along the way, many Bible verses will be cited as support for the statements and ideas found within this book. This is so that readers can choose to follow the recommended practice of looking up the verses in the Bible or an online Bible app, to read the verses in their contexts in order to decide whether the verse truly supports the author's claims (Acts 17:11). However, this sort of in-depth study may be best to do on a subsequent read-through of this book, so that the reader's flow of thought is not interrupted as concepts are being introduced and explained for the first time.

Most of the discussion in this book will support the perspective that Jesus will suddenly take all Christians to be with him in Heaven in an event called *the Rapture*, which will occur before the beginning of the seven years of divine judgments that the world will experience during the Tribulation. The Tribulation will end with the *Second Coming* of Jesus Christ. Jesus will then personally rule the entire world for a thousand years, in what is called Jesus' *Millennial Kingdom*.

However, before going into detail on this perspective, the first chapter of this book will examine a few other perspectives on the timing of Jesus' Second Coming in relation to Jesus' Millennial Kingdom. This discussion will be helpful in order to understand why the perspective taken in this book is the most consistent and straight-forward understanding of end-times Bible prophecy.

The following chapters will cover different aspects of the end times, including:

- The event called the Rapture, and when it will occur.
- Signs that indicate the Tribulation is approaching.

- The twenty-one divine judgments that the world will experience during the Tribulation.
- Two individuals who will have great power over the world during the Tribulation: the *Antichrist* and the *False Prophet.*
- The *Mark of the Beast* that people will need to accept in order to be able to buy or sell anything during the Tribulation, and why this Mark must be avoided at all costs.
- The main purposes of the Tribulation, which will all be achieved at the Second Coming of Jesus.
- The thousand-year Millennial Kingdom that Jesus will set up after he returns to Earth.

Finally, the Appendix will discuss a few remaining questions about some details of Bible prophecy that are still debated among prophecy experts, such as the Psalm 83 War, the Gog-Magog War, and the future of the United States of America.

All of this information, however, ultimately does not matter unless it is spiritually beneficial to the individual who has learned it. Thus, the final chapter of this book will discuss what the coming end times mean for your life and your relationship to Jesus Christ right now.

Chapter 1

Different Perspectives of the End Times

What the Bible teaches about the end times has always been a debateable topic. There are several different frameworks that Christians use to interpret the many Bible verses that are related to end-times prophecies.

Biblical interpretation is complex, because the Bible was written by dozens of different human authors over a span of thousands of years, in three different ancient languages: Hebrew, Greek, and Aramaic. Despite this diversity, the Bible consistently tells the same message about how God interacts with humanity.

The main narrative told throughout the Bible is the story of a loving and holy God who created the whole universe and everything in it. God made people so that they could live in loving relationships with God and with one another.

However, people turned away from God, and sinned by disobeying God's instructions for how he wants people to live, because people always think their own way is better. Ultimately, though, these sins only lead to suffering, death, and God's eternal judgment.

Despite their sinful disobedience, God did not give up on humanity. Instead, God sent his only eternal Son to be born into the world where he would live as a man and die for humanity's sins.

By dying on the cross, Jesus suffered the punishment of death that God's holy justice requires for all sinners. Now, everyone who believes that Jesus Christ died for their sins instantly has their sins forgiven by God, so that they can once again have a personal relationship with God that will last forever.

Numerous portions of the Bible also contain prophecies, which are predictions for the future that were made by human prophets who were inspired by God (2 Peter 1:21), as well as Jesus Christ himself. Many of these prophecies were fulfilled in the past, close to when the prophets first spoke about them. The prophets who made these predictions were held to very high standards, because if their prophecies did not come true, they could be executed (Deuteronomy 18:20–22).

But some of these prophets also spoke about things that would happen in the distant future, sometimes hundreds or thousands of years from when the prophets themselves lived.

For example, many prophecies were fulfilled by Jesus Christ's First Coming to Earth. Prophets correctly predicted the details about his miraculous birth, such as that his mother Mary would be a virgin at the time of Jesus' birth (Isaiah 7:14). Other prophecies predicted the places that Jesus lived as a child (Micah 5:2, Matthew 2:14–15, 2:23), and foretold what Jesus would teach about and do during his three-year earthly ministry (Luke 4:16–21).

Jesus' crucifixion for sin, and his subsequent death and physical resurrection, which occurred around the year 33 AD fulfilled even more prophecies (e.g., Isaiah 53, Genesis 3:15).

These fulfilled prophecies and the eyewitness testimonies to Jesus' bodily resurrection and ascension to Heaven are the reason Christians believe that Jesus Christ was both fully God and a human being simultaneously. His unique dual nature is why Christians believe that Jesus is able to give eternal life to everyone who believes in him as their Savior (e.g., John 3:16).

However, as amazing as Jesus' First Coming was because of what his death and resurrection achieved for humanity, there are still many prophecies that do not seem to have been fulfilled yet. This is why most

Christians believe that Jesus is coming back to Earth sometime again in the future, so that all the prophecies in the Bible will finally be fulfilled.

Although many Christians would agree that every prophecy in the Bible is true and will be fulfilled one day, there is strong debate over when and how Christians should expect these prophecies to be fulfilled.

THREE MAIN POSITIONS ON JESUS' SECOND COMING AND HIS MILLENNIAL KINGDOM

Regarding the timing of Jesus' Second Coming, there are usually three main positions taken by Christians. Each of these positions are related to a specific time that is prophesied in the Bible called Jesus' *Millennial Kingdom*, or simply, *the Millennium*.

These three positions are:

1. That Jesus will not literally have a Millennial Kingdom on Earth (i.e., *amillennialism*).
2. That Jesus will return to Earth before he sets up his literal Millennial Kingdom that will last for a thousand years (i.e., *premillennialism*).
3. That Jesus will return to Earth only after Christianity has spread throughout the whole world. As a result, the world will have been brought to a near-utopian state of peace and righteousness

which is identified as Jesus' Millennial Kingdom (i.e., *postmillennialism*).

These three positions will now be discussed in more detail, to introduce some of the technical terms used by experts in discussions of Bible prophecy.

The position called *amillennialism* claims that Jesus will not literally set up a Millennial Kingdom. Amillennialists do not think that Jesus will literally rule on earth for a thousand years after his Second Coming.

Those who support this *amillennial* position only expect that Jesus will return to Earth at some point in the future at his Second Coming. Then, everyone will be resurrected. Jesus will determine who will have eternal life in the New Heavens and New Earth, and who will face eternal destruction in the Lake of Fire (Revelation 20:11–15).

The position called *postmillennialism* clams that Jesus will not return to earth until after Jesus' Millennial Kingdom has occurred.

Usually, postmillennialists believe that Christianity will spread around the world and help everyone's lives become progressively better. Once the world has reached a high level of peace and righteousness, then Jesus will return to resurrect and judge everyone to determine if they will have eternal life or eternal death.

The position that is taken by this book is called *premillennialism*. In this view, Jesus' Second Coming will occur before his Millennial Kingdom.

Advocates of this position expect that Jesus will return and then set up a literal kingdom. He will reign over a world that is full of peace and righteousness for at least a thousand years, with the help of his saints (Revelation 20:4–5).

Note that, throughout this book, the term "saints" is not referring only to a few special Christians who lived especially holy lives. Instead, "saints" refers to all people who believed in God or Jesus throughout history. So all Christians are saints, but there were also Israelite/Jewish saints, and even saints in the time before Israel existed. There will be even more people who become saints during the Tribulation.

Each position described above takes a different approach to interpreting Bible prophecies, and in particular, to the biblical Book of Revelation and the events that it describes.

Amillennialism and the Spiritual View of Revelation

Amillennialists mostly deny that the Book of Revelation is about real events that will occur in the world, whether in the future or in the past.

To support their position, amillennialists interpret the Book of Revelation and other prophetic passages of Scripture that talk about the end times *allegorically* or spiritually, rather than literally.

For example, amillennialists might believe that the Book of Revelation is only talking about the spiritual war between good and evil that has been going on between God and Satan for thousands of years.

Satan was initially a high-ranking angel named Lucifer. Angels are purely spiritual beings that were created by God to be ministers to humanity (Hebrews 1:13–14). However, at some point in the past, Lucifer became the devil when he chose to rebel against God (Ezekiel 28:11–19, Isaiah 14:12–15). One third of the angels sided with him, and they became known as *demons* (Revelation 12:4–12). In Hebrew, *Satan* means *the adversary* or *the enemy*.

Amillennialists usually claim that the main point made in the Book of Revelation is that God and God's people will be victorious in the end, when Satan and all his demons and God-rejecting people will be destroyed. Similarly, Amillennialists might interpret Jesus' Millennial Kingdom as the spiritual reign of Jesus in the hearts of Christians.

Christians who support postmillennialism or premillennialism will be able to agree with some of these amillennialists' claims. God and his people will ultimately be victorious over evil and Satan, and ideally,

Jesus Christ should currently be reigning in Christians' hearts. Jesus reigns in individual believers' hearts when they try to live in ways that are pleasing to him, obeying him as their Lord.

Yet unlike the other perspectives on the end-times, amillennialism does not expect the details of the Book of Revelation to be fulfilled literally, whether at some point in the future, or at some point in the past.

Amillennialism became popular early on in Christian history, thanks to influential Bible interpreters and theologians who preferred to interpret many parts of Scripture allegorically.

Some of these early interpreters were concerned that the idea of a literal kingdom of God on Earth was too unspiritual. They thought a literal interpretation of Bible prophecies regarding Jesus' Millennial Kingdom risked making the glorious kingdom of God into something carnal and earthly. For example, the idea of people having literal feasts and eating real food in resurrected physical bodies was seen as unacceptable.

These early Bible interpreters who used allegorical interpretation were likely influenced by Greek philosophy that claimed the physical world was corrupt or partly evil. Christians who appreciated Greek philosophy wanted to imagine that Jesus would have a purely spiritual kingdom that would be untainted by physical reality.

Yet the Bible says that God created the physical world, and that it was good (Genesis 1:31). It was only after the first sin was committed by Adam and Eve that God's physical creation was temporarily placed under a curse, and death came into the world (Genesis 3, Romans 5:12–14). At the end of history, Christians will live on the New Earth, in resurrected and glorified immortal physical bodies, in a beautiful city called the New Jerusalem. All of it will be perfect and untainted by sin in any way (Revelation 21).

So there is no need for Christians to rely on allegorical interpretation in order to preserve God's holiness or transcendence, because God is the one who chose to create the physical world, and to even have his Son become a human man named Jesus Christ. Jesus will have a physical human body forever, just like all resurrected humans will (Philippians 3:20–21). There is no such thing as a non-physical bodily resurrection.

Therefore, Christians should have no theological objection to the idea of Jesus having a literal kingdom for a thousand years in this world, if that is what God desires to do. The only question for debate is whether the Bible teaches that this is actually what God wants to do.

Postmillennialism and the Preterist and Historicist Views of Revelation

Because postmillennialists believe that Jesus will only return after the world has experienced a long period of peace and righteousness, they also have to interpret large portions of the Book of Revelation allegorically, rather than literally.

To support their interpretation of Jesus' Millennial Kingdom, postmillennialists generally hold to one of two different positions on the Book of Revelation. These two positions are called *preterism* and *historicism*.

Preterism is the position that most Bible prophecies about the end times were fulfilled by the year 70 AD, when the Romans invaded Jerusalem, destroying the city and the second Temple.

Yet preterists usually still believe that at some point in the future, Jesus will return to resurrect and judge everyone. Following this, God will destroy the current universe and create the New Heaven and New Earth, while preserving the resurrected bodies of all of his redeemed saints (Revelation 21:1, 2 Peter 3:10–13, Matthew 24:35).

Some extreme preterists go so far as to argue that Jesus *did* return in 70 AD, and that ever since then the world has been experiencing Jesus' Millennial Kingdom, or maybe even the New Heaven and New Earth!

However, it is difficult to believe this claim when there is still so much suffering, violence, sin, and death occurring all around the world.

There are many verses throughout the Old Testament that say that in Jesus' Millennial Kingdom, the world will be much better than it has ever been before, except for perhaps in the Garden of Eden, before anyone had sinned (e.g., Amos 9:13–15, Isaiah 11:6–8, Isaiah 35).

Furthermore, for extreme preterists to claim that all God's promises of resurrection and eternal life for those who believe in Jesus are being experienced now by Christians in this world is frankly unbelievable. Many Christians have been tortured and killed for their faith in horrible ways over the last two thousand years. Paul clearly says that Christians should be pitied if they only have hope for this life, and do not believe in a future bodily resurrection (1 Corinthians 15:12–19).

Preterism may appeal to Christians who prefer an allegorical approach to Scripture, like that taken by many of the early church's most notable theologians. Preterism may also appeal to Christians who do not like to speculate or worry about the end times.

Preterism could be compatible with either amillennial or postmillennial perspectives on Jesus' Second Coming. Yet premillennialists and even many postmillennialists find the preterist view rather unconvincing.

One major reason for this is because preterists generally have to interpret large sections of the Book of Revelation allegorically, rather than literally. Interpreters who do this often ignore the specific details about the divine judgments that are given throughout the Book of Revelation chapters 6 to 19. In contrast, premillennialists typically pay close attention to the details that are given in these chapters of Scripture.

Also, although it is debated, there is good evidence that the Book of Revelation was written perhaps as late as 96 AD, decades *after* the Roman invasion and destruction of Jerusalem. If this is true, then it would not have made sense for John to claim that the things he wrote about in Revelation would soon take place (Revelation 1:1), because everything he wrote about would have been mostly fulfilled decades before he began to write!

Therefore, many Bible interpreters argue that when John was writing the Book of Revelation, he really *was* writing about things that were still yet to come from his perspective. If this is true, it eliminates preterism as a plausible interpretive option, which means that interpreters must endorse either a *historicist* or *futurist* perspective of the Book of Revelation.

Historicism is the perspective that the twenty-one judgments described in the Book of Revelation chapters 6 to 19 have mostly occurred throughout history, although there may be some judgments that will still be fulfilled in the future.

Like the preterists, historicist interpreters of the Book of Revelation tend to allegorize the divine judgments and ignore some of their details in order to make the judgments fit with particular historical events that have occurred since the times of the early church.

The historicist perspective may be attractive to those who expect Jesus to return only after Christians have significantly improved the moral, spiritual, and physical condition of the world (i.e., postmillennialists). Historicism may also appeal to Bible interpreters who argue that the Rapture occurs at the end of the Tribulation.

However, the weakness of the preterist and historicist perspectives is that because they rely on allegorical interpretation, almost every interpreter has a different perspective on which historical events supposedly fulfilled these judgments.

This inconsistent method of interpretation does not make the Book of Revelation very useful for its readers of any era. If the events described in Revelation already happened in the past, then they do not have any relevance for Christians either today or in the future.

Premillennialism and the Futurist View of Revelation

Premillennialism is the idea that Jesus will return at his Second Coming to set up his Millennial Kingdom on Earth.

This position fits best with a futurist reading of the Book of Revelation. Futurists claim that most of the events described after Revelation chapter 3 will be fulfilled in the future.

In contrast to preterist and historicist perspectives on the Book of Revelation, it is only the *futurist* perspective that pays close attention to the details of the end-times judgments that John prophesied will occur.

Futurist interpreters also take most of the details of these twenty-one divine judgments literally, unless it is clear that John is speaking symbolically. For example, futurists do not believe that a real red dragon or a literal beast with seven heads and ten horns will rule the world in Revelation 13. However, futurists believe these symbols represent real individuals who will fulfill the actions that are attributed to them through the use of these symbols.

The strength of the futurist perspective is that, generally, interpreters who take this view can consistently agree with one another about what parts of the Book of Revelation are symbolic, and what parts should be taken literally.

Futurist interpreters also tend to be fairly consistent with one another regarding what the symbolic parts of the Book of Revelation are describing, and what the divine judgments described in Revelation chapters 6 to 19 will involve.

This interpretive consistency has led to the formation of networks of prophecy watchers, scholars, commentators, and pastors who teach about the Book of Revelation in very similar ways, although there are still minor disagreements regarding some details.

These experts share their premillennial perspectives through organizing prophecy conferences, writing books and Internet articles, or recording videos. They often appear on one another's radio or television shows and Internet podcasts to discuss how current events relate to Bible prophecy. They may also enjoy speculating about how soon they believe the events of the Book of Revelation may be fulfilled.

However, there is occasional disagreement even among futurists regarding the timing of a major end-times event called the Rapture in relation to the events of the Tribulation. This issue will be discussed more in the next chapter.

Because the futurist perspective takes the details of the judgments in the Book of Revelation seriously and refuses to gloss over them with allegorical interpretation, it means that if the futurist perspective is correct, then the Book of Revelation will be very useful to those people who will actually live through these particular events.

These people should be able to identify where the world is in regard to the sequence of the twenty-one divine judgments, and therefore prepare themselves for what will be coming next, to the best of their ability. They should also be able to know how much longer it will be before Jesus will return at his Second Coming.

Premillennial futurism, which teaches that the Rapture will happen before the Tribulation, also provides motivation for Christians today to share the gospel with people they know, in hope that these people will believe in Jesus and therefore be raptured instead of having to live through the awful events of the Tribulation.

On the other hand, critics of the futurist perspective believe that speculation about the end times is dangerous. In particular, critics claim it leads to disappointment and skepticism when Christians set particular dates for when Jesus is expected to return, and the date goes by without anything happening.

Many futurist interpreters are careful to avoid setting specific dates for the Rapture or Jesus' Second Coming for this exact reason. Only a few futurists try to look for particular timelines that align important end-times events with key Jewish feast dates on particular years, for example.

Other critics will point to the ever-changing list of candidates that futurists claim could potentially become the Antichrist or the False Prophet. However, usually most futurists say that it is impossible to know for sure who these individuals will be until the Tribulation begins.

Many critics of the futurist perspective will also claim that Christians who look for signs of the end times are perversely excited by doom and gloom, or that they are using fear to scare people into believing in Jesus.

In response to these critics, those Christians who take the futurist approach to the end times argue that they are simply doing what Jesus commanded when he told his followers to stay awake and watch for the signs of his return (Matthew 24:42–44, Mark 13:32–37, Luke 21:34–36, Revelation 3:3). Futurists also often feel called to warn others about the risk of being left behind at the Rapture to face God's judgment (Ezekiel 33:2–6).

One way of determining which of the above perspectives on the end times is the most likely to be correct is to look at what the Bible says the world will be like as it approaches the end times.

For example, postmillennialists claim that Jesus will only return after Christianity gradually spreads around the world and makes the world better and better. Therefore, if postmillennialism is true, then after two thousand years since Jesus' ascension into Heaven, the world should be becoming better and more righteous than it was at the time of the early church.

Yet today, it can be argued that Christianity has never been more persecuted and hated, even in comparison to the hostility to Christianity that was experienced by the early church. Many societies that were once friendly to Christianity and the gospel are becoming increasingly secular and hostile to Christian values.

Even many supposedly-Christian pastors are no longer preaching the true gospel, but are preaching sermons that ignore or even condone sin in order to make their audience feel good about themselves, instead of encouraging their audience to avoid sin and believe in Jesus Christ for eternal life.

Premillennialists argue that the increasing hostility toward Christianity, and the watering-down of the gospel message are just a few of the signs that Christians should expect to see if the world is truly approaching the time of the Tribulation.

Paradoxically, then, as Christians watch the world around them become spiritually darker and feel their lives becoming more difficult, they can be encouraged that seeing these signs means that the Rapture will be happening soon, because the Biblical evidence shows that the Rapture will happen before the seven-year Tribulation.

Chapter 2

The Rapture and Its Timing

The Rapture is the next major event that will occur in regard to Bible prophecy.

There will be a sound of a trumpet, the voice of an angel, and a commanding shout that might say, "Come up here!"

Jesus himself will appear in the clouds, and he will resurrect all deceased people who had believed in him at some point during their lifetimes.

Next, everyone who is still alive that has believed in Jesus at some point during their lifetimes will also be called up to join Jesus and these resurrected people in the clouds.

All of this is based on 1 Thessalonians 4:16–17, Revelation 4:1, and Revelation 11:12.

As shorthand, prophecy experts simply call this event *the Rapture*. Sometimes it is called *the Rapture of the Church*, to specify that it will involve all Christians, regardless of whether they are alive or dead at the moment it occurs.

During the Rapture, both the resurrected formerly-deceased Christians and the caught-up living Christians will have their bodies instantly transformed to become like Jesus' glorious body. This means their bodies will become perfect, immortal, and imperishable (1 Corinthians 15:49–53).

Other traits of these glorified bodies include that they will be beautiful, handsome, and strong. They will no longer be "natural" bodies made of flesh and blood, but will be "spiritual" bodies (1 Corinthians 15:42–50). The Bible does not say what these spiritual bodies will be made of, or how they will work in every detail.

However, because the Bible says these bodies will be like Jesus' glorified body (1 Corinthians 15:49), these spiritual bodies will likely include abilities like what Jesus demonstrated after his resurrection. This included the ability to appear and disappear at will (Luke 24:31), and even suddenly appear inside a locked room without using the door (John 20:19, 20:26). Yet Jesus was not a ghost, because he could still eat, people could physically touch him, and he was recognizable as himself (Luke 24:36–43, John 20:27, Luke 24:30–31). So similarly, people's resurrected and glorified bodies will be recognizable as themselves, but significantly upgraded in terms of appearance and abilities.

Currently, natural human bodies are only like flimsy tents that people live in temporarily. In contrast, these new glorified bodies will be strong and eternal, like a beautiful building made of strong materials that will never degrade (2 Corinthians 5:1–5). Christians long for the day when this transformation will occur, which the Apostle Paul referred to as the redemption of their bodies (Romans 8:23).

After meeting Jesus in the clouds, raptured Christians will go with Jesus to Heaven, where he has been preparing places for them to live in his Father's house (John 14:1–3).

Christians are told to look forward to when Jesus will appear for the Rapture, because it is their blessed hope (Titus 2:13). It is something that gives Christians peace (John 14:1–3), and Christians should encourage each other by reminding each other about the coming Rapture (1 Thessalonians 4:18, 5:10–11).

Critics claim that the word *Rapture* is not in the Bible. This is true. None of the verses cited earlier used this exact English word. But as shown, the event itself is clearly described in a number of Bible verses.

Every word of Scripture was given by the divine inspiration of the Holy Spirit to the human authors (2 Timothy 3:16, 2 Peter 1:21, John 14:26). Therefore, the verses listed above *will* be fulfilled at some point. It is not true to say that the Rapture will never happen.

The objection that the word *Rapture* is not in the Bible is similar to how other important Christian terms are not found in the Bible, either.

For example, the word *Trinity* is not in the Bible, but it is a core doctrine of Christian faith, because it is used to describe how God is one divine being but three persons: Father, Son, and Holy Spirit (e.g., Matthew 3:16–17).

Even the word *Bible* is not found in the Bible! So this fact that any particular word is not found in Scripture does not mean that the concepts that have come to be known by these words are automatically false or unbiblical.

The English term *rapture* actually comes from the Latin word *rapere*. In 1 Thessalonians 4:17, *rapere* was used to translate the original Greek verb *harpazo*. *Harpazo* means to catch up or snatch away, perhaps even suddenly and with force.

Additionally, for Christians, the Rapture truly will be an event that brings them ecstasy, bliss, and joy, as in English definitions of the word *rapture*.

When Will the Rapture Happen?

Now that the Biblical basis for the event that is called the Rapture has been established, the next most important question is when the Rapture will occur. This is an issue that is hotly debated.

The three main positions regarding when the Rapture will occur say that it will happen:

1. Before the Tribulation begins (i.e., *pre-Tribulation*).
2. Sometime near the half-way point of the Tribulation (i.e., *mid-Tribulation*).
3. At the end of the Tribulation, at the same time as when Jesus returns to Earth at his Second Coming (i.e., *post-Tribulation*).

However, only one of the above options can be true. To determine which one is true, the arguments for each position must be examined.

The Post-Tribulation Rapture Position

Those who support the post-Tribulation Rapture position say that it is simplest to identify the Rapture with the Second Coming of Jesus Christ to Earth. That way, there is no need to separate the Rapture and Jesus' Second Coming into two different events that are potentially years apart.

Some Bible commentators who support the post-Tribulation position refer to ancient middle-east traditions of when a king would return from battle. The people of the city would go out to meet their victorious king when they saw him coming in the distance, and then celebrate as they return in a parade back to their city with their king.

Post-Tribulation Rapture supporters apply this concept to Jesus' Second Coming. They argue that the Rapture will happen at the end of the Tribulation, when Jesus appears in the clouds on his white horse (Revelation 19:11).

They say that at Jesus' Second Coming, Christians will be called up into the clouds to meet Jesus there. Then, Christians will immediately return with Jesus for the Battle of Armageddon, and the celebration that will happen afterward at the Marriage Supper of the Lamb.

Possible biblical support for this interpretation comes from verses that say when Jesus returns in the clouds at the end of the Tribulation, he will send angels to gather all of the people who belong to him everywhere in the world (Mark 13:24–27, Matthew 24:29–31).

Yet there is a more plausible interpretation of these verses than the Rapture.

Generally, Christians who believe in the Rapture (whether pre-Tribulation, mid-Tribulation, or post-

Tribulation) accept the idea that after Jesus' Second Coming, Jesus will set up a literal kingdom based in Jerusalem. From there, Jesus will rule the world for over a thousand years with the help of his saints.

However, before his Millennial Kingdom can be established, Jesus must judge all of the people who will survive the Tribulation. The purpose of this judgment is to determine who will be allowed to enter Jesus' kingdom (Matthew 25:31–46). It is called the Sheep and Goats Judgment.

But, if the post-Tribulation Rapture position were correct, and the Rapture happened at Jesus' Second Coming, there would be no reason to have this judgment. That is because anyone who was a Christian would have already been raptured and transformed from mortal to immortal when Jesus returned to Earth. Yet if this happened, it would lead to a major problem for Jesus' Millennial Kingdom.

The problem would be because after the Rapture, everyone who is resurrected and/or raptured will no longer be married to anyone, or go on to marry anyone in the future (Luke 20:34–36, Mark 12:25, Matthew 22:30). Therefore, it is also presumed that everyone who will have been raptured will not go on to have children, because it is a sin to have sex outside of marriage (Hebrews 13:4).

So, if the Rapture happened at Jesus' Second Coming, then only unbelievers would be left on Earth in their mortal bodies. Thus, only these unbelievers would be able to marry and have children to repopulate the world.

However, all the unbelievers who rejected Jesus during the Tribulation will not make it through the Sheep and Goats Judgment. Instead, they will be thrown into the Lake of Fire (Matthew 25:41, 13:36–43, Isaiah 66:24).

Thus, if the Rapture were to happen at the end of the Tribulation, then no one would be left alive after the Sheep and Goats Judgment who would be able to marry or have children, and so repopulate the world.

That would mean there would be no one for Jesus and his saints to rule over, like they are promised they will in many different places in the Bible (e.g., Revelation 20:4, Luke 19:17–19, 2 Timothy 2:12).

Additionally, if the Rapture happened after the Tribulation, then no one who was left alive after the Sheep and Goats Judgment would be able to be an unbeliever.

But the Bible says that a very large number of unbelievers will take part in a final rebellion at the end of Jesus' Millennial Kingdom. This rebellion will be thanks to the prompting of Satan. He will be released again for a short period of time from the bottomless pit, and so be allowed back to Earth to tempt people to rebel against Jesus once more (Revelation 20:7–10).

The only place that these rebellious unbelievers could come from is if they were the descendants of mortal people who survived the Tribulation and were permitted entry into Jesus' Millennial Kingdom. These people would then go on to have children and repopulate the world, leading to a great number of people who could choose to rebel at the end of Jesus' thousand-year reign.

Therefore, it seems that the Bible itself rules out the possibility of a post-Tribulation Rapture, unless there is no literal thousand-year reign of Christ, and no final rebellion against him.

But to take such a position requires interpreters to ignore many Bible verses, or else interpret the verses about these events allegorically. Yet allegorical interpretation is not a consistent approach to Biblical interpretation, as discussed in Chapter 1.

THE MID-TRIBULATION RAPTURE POSITION

Those who believe in a Mid-Tribulation Rapture usually identify the trumpet of God that accompanies the Rapture (1 Thessalonians 4:16) with the seventh trumpet blown by an angel to announce the beginning of God's fourteenth judgment of the Tribulation (Revelation 11:15).

The Mid-Tribulation Rapture is sometimes also called a Pre-Wrath Rapture, because its supporters argue that the world only experiences God's wrath during the final seven judgments in Revelation chapter 16.

It is true that Christians who are alive today are told that they will not experience God's wrath (1 Thessalonians 5:9, Romans 5:9) because God's wrath is only meant for rebellious unbelievers (e.g., John 3:36, Ephesians 2:3, Romans 1:18, 2:8). Therefore, Jesus will save Christians who live before the Rapture from experiencing the wrath that God will subject the world to during the Tribulation (1 Thessalonians 1:10).

However, it is false to say that during the Tribulation, God's wrath only begins after the fourteenth judgment. God's wrath is actually mentioned much earlier on in the sequence of divine judgments during the Tribulation, such as in the sixth judgment (Revelation 6:16).

Even the first four judgments are devastating for the world. By the end of the fourth judgment, up to one quarter of the entire Earth's population might have been killed by war, famine, disease, and other causes (Revelation 6:8). So it is false to say that God only begins to subject the world to his wrath after the fourteenth judgment.

Furthermore, the entire seven years of the Tribulation are sometimes called the *Day of the Lord*, which is a specific period of time that is associated with God's wrath and the return of Jesus to Earth (2 Peter 3:10, 1

Thessalonians 5:1–3). Yet another verse clearly promises that God will keep Christians who believe in him before the Rapture out of the entire seven years of the Tribulation (Revelation 3:10).

Therefore, a Mid-Tribulation Rapture seems to be eliminated as a possibility on the basis of Scripture itself.

THE PRE-TRIBULATION RAPTURE POSITION

As seen in the earlier portions of this chapter, advocates of the Pre-Tribulation Rapture find several problems with both the Post-Tribulation and Mid-Tribulation Rapture positions.

Pre-Tribulation Rapture supporters also have several strong arguments for why the Rapture will happen before the Tribulation begins.

For example, the Rapture is described as a blessed hope for Christians (Titus 2:13). It is something that should give Christians peace (John 14:1–3). Christians should encourage each other by reminding each other about the coming Rapture (1 Thessalonians 4:18, 5:10–11).

But if the Rapture will only happen in the middle or at the end of the Tribulation, then it is difficult to use the Rapture as a way to encourage Christians who are currently living on Earth, because of how awful the Tribulation will be. It would not be an encouragement or a source of peace for someone to expect to experience any part of God's twenty-one judgments that are described in the Book of Revelation.

Jesus said the Tribulation will be the worst time in the entire history of the world. If Jesus did not return to end it when he does, no one would survive (Mark 13:19–20, Matthew 24:21–22). When the people of the world realize that the Tribulation has begun, many will faint out of fear, and some of their hearts will fail (Luke 21:26).

So it makes sense that Christians would hope to be raptured before the Tribulation, rather than having to experience some or all of the disastrous things that the Bible says will happen during the Tribulation.

In relation to this last point, the Bible actually mentions a group of Christians who were worried that they had entered the Tribulation, but the Apostle Paul reassured them that this was not true (2 Thessalonians 2:1–2).

It seems that if Paul had taught these Christians that they should expect to go through the Tribulation, they would not have been so fearful. Instead, they should have accepted it as something to expect before Jesus' Second Coming. The fact that they were alarmed suggests that they did not expect they would have to face the Tribulation.

Paul calmed these Christians' fears by reminding them of how a particular event still had to happen before the Antichrist could be revealed at the beginning of the Tribulation.

In the original Greek, this event is referred to as *he apostasia* (2 Thessalonians 2:3). Many English Bibles translate *he apostasia* as "the apostasy," "the falling away," or "the rebellion."

As a result, it is commonly thought that Paul is referring to a time when many Christians will lose their faith, or a time when many societies will turn away from Christianity.

There are several other Bible verses that suggest the Church will struggle with false teachers and false doctrines in the end times (e.g., 1 Timothy 4:1–3, 2 Timothy 4:3–4, 2 Peter 2:1–3). Jesus himself warned that many in the end times will "fall away" from their faith, and then go on to betray each other (Matthew 24:10).

Yet there have been false teachers and false doctrines around ever since the time of the early church. There have also been various times in history when Christians faced persecution and some of them fell away from their faith, or betrayed each other.

Today, Christian faith is slowly declining in countries that formerly had large numbers of Christians. The number of Christians in these countries are also expected to decline further in the future.

But Christianity is growing in other areas of the world. So it is difficult to say that this "falling away" from Christian faith will be such an identifiable event that Christians will be able to watch for it as a sign to determine whether they have entered the Tribulation or not.

However, *he apostasia* in 2 Thessalonians 2:3 can also be translated more literally as "the departure." In fact, one of the earliest English Bible translations (the 1599 Geneva Bible) chose to translate it this way.

When translated this way, then this verse would be a clear reference to the Rapture. What greater "departure" will there be than the moment when all Christians will literally leave this world and go to be with Jesus in Heaven?

If this is what Paul meant by the term *he apostasia*, then it would be a clear statement that Christians should expect the Rapture to happen before the Tribulation.

Additionally, the Rapture will certainly be an identifiable event that no one could miss, unlike an undefined period of time when people gradually fall away from Christian faith.

Furthermore, remember that Paul had taught the Thessalonians about the Rapture in his first letter to them (1 Thessalonians chapter 4). If the Thessalonian Christians believed they had missed the Rapture and so would have to face the Tribulation, then it explains why they were so anxious. It also explains why Paul would comfort them by reminding them that the Rapture must happen first before the Tribulation will begin.

The idea that Christians who are alive before the Rapture will not enter into the Tribulation is reinforced by Revelation 3:10. In this verse, Jesus promises faithful Christians who are alive before the Tribulation that he will return to keep them out of the time of the coming trials that the whole world will experience.

If the Rapture happens before the Tribulation, then Revelation 3:10 makes sense. Instead of being on Earth during the Tribulation, Christians will be in Heaven with Jesus, in the places he prepared for them in the Father's house (John 14:1–3).

If Jesus had only wanted to promise Christians that he would protect and provide for them as they lived *through* the Tribulation, he could have clearly said this. For example, in the Old Testament, God protected his faithful people from being killed even when Jerusalem was surrounded and invaded by enemy armies (Ezekiel 9).

Yet instead of promising Christians something like this divine protection during the Tribulation, Jesus promises in Revelation 3:10 that these Christians will not even be *in* this future time of divine judgment.

However, this does not mean that there will be *no* Christians on Earth during the Tribulation. Actually, there will be a great revival of Christianity during the beginning of the Tribulation!

Many non-Christians who will be left behind after the Rapture will recognize what has happened, and they will realize their mistake of not accepting Jesus as their Savior before the Rapture. Then they will believe in Jesus and gain eternal life, but they will also have to face severe persecution and possible death during the Tribulation (Revelation 6:9–11, 7:9–14, 20:4).

It will be difficult, but some of these new Christians will survive until the end of the Tribulation and will be alive at Jesus' Second Coming. It is they who will pass Jesus' Sheep and Goats judgment (Matthew 25:31–46), and therefore go on to marry and repopulate the world during Jesus' Millennial Kingdom.

Bible interpreters can also see that Jesus was alluding to the Rapture when he talked about a time when two men will be working in the same field, but one will be taken and one left behind. Or two women will be grinding grain at the same mill, but one will be taken and the other one left behind (Matthew 24:40–44).

Evidence for this interpretation of Matthew 24:40–44 comes from how the word translated as "taken" in this verse is the Greek verb *paralambano*. *Paralambano* means to receive someone to oneself, or to take a person along with someone, or for someone to be carried off.

Paralambano is also the same verb used in John 14:3, when Jesus promised his disciples that he would return to take them to the Father's house. This is exactly what will happen at the Rapture, when Jesus appears in the clouds to take all Christians to Heaven with him.

What is also interesting is that the verb *paralambano* is used in Matthew 1:20, when an angel tells Joseph to not be afraid to take Mary as his wife.

Many pre-Tribulation Rapture proponents point out that the Church, made up of all true believers in Jesus, is called the Bride of Christ (e.g., Revelation 19:7, 21:9–10, 22:17). Paul explained that human marriage is an analogy of Jesus Christ's relationship to the Church (Ephesians 5:25–32).

During Jesus' earthly life, in the region of Galilee, it was traditional for a woman to become engaged to a man but continue to live in her parents' home for up to a year before the wedding would occur. The groom would return to his father's house, and begin to construct a room for himself and the bride to live in after being married.

Once the groom's father decided that it was time, and had determined that the bride's new room had been built sufficiently well, he would tell the groom to go retrieve the bride.

It was common for this to be a surprising event, when the groom and his friends might show up at the bride's home in the middle of the night with torches, and they would joyfully shout that the groom was coming. The bride had to be prepared to go at any time, and she eagerly anticipated the day when her groom would come and her wedding would occur.

Some commentators even suggest that the bride would be lifted up and carried along by this wedding party, who would take her back to the groom's home. There, the bride and groom would stay for seven days in the new chamber the groom had built, where they would consummate their marriage.

When the seven days were finished, the new married couple would come out of their chamber, and the entire community would celebrate with a wedding feast. Such a feast was the location of Jesus' first miracle (John 2:1–11).

Pre-Tribulation Rapture supporters cannot help but see the same pattern of a Galilean wedding in the timing of the Rapture. This could even be exactly what Jesus was implying when he told his disciples that he would go away to prepare dwelling places for them, and then return to take them to be with him in the Father's house (John 14:1–3).

Jesus referred to himself as a bridegroom (Mark 2:19–20, Luke 5:34–35). He also told a parable involving a king who invited people to a wedding feast, as a metaphor of Jesus' Millennial Kingdom (Matthew 22:1–14). John the Baptist considered himself to be a friend of the bridegroom, referring to Jesus (John 3:29).

Some commentators highlight other instances in the Old Testament of Israelite/Jewish men who got married to Gentile (i.e., non-Israelite/non-Jewish) women, and see these as foreshadowing of Jesus' marriage to the mostly-Gentile Church. Historically, the Church is composed of far more non-Jewish Christians than Jewish Christians.

For example, the Old Testament Book of Ruth tells about Boaz. He was an Israelite man who married Ruth, a Moabite woman. Ruth was the widowed daughter-in-law of Naomi, who was an Israelite. Ruth had faithfully come back to Israel to care for Naomi after both their husbands died in Moab, and Boaz was also related to Naomi. After marrying Ruth, Boaz redeemed Naomi's land that, according to the law at the time, could only be bought back by someone in Naomi's family tree.

Boaz can thus be seen as a *type*, or a foreshadowing, of Jesus Christ. Jesus will also redeem Israel's land, by coming to claim it and restore all of it to Israel at the Second Coming (Acts 1:6). But before this, he will spiritually marry a mostly-Gentile bride, which is the Church.

There is also the example of Joseph, one of the twelve sons of Jacob. After being sold into slavery in Egypt, Joseph eventually warned the Pharaoh of a coming seven-year famine, which can be seen as a foreshadowing of the seven-year Tribulation (Genesis 41:25–36).

After Joseph had been appointed as second-in-command to the Pharaoh, he married an Egyptian woman before the awful seven-year famine came (Genesis 41:45). Similarly, Jesus will also marry his bride, the Church, before the seven-year Tribulation.

There are other *types* or foreshadowing of the Rapture in the Old Testament, where God rescued those who trusted in him from experiencing impending harm or death.

For example, Enoch was taken up to Heaven before the Flood, which God saved Noah and his family through by telling them to build a large wooden boat (Genesis 5:24, Hebrews 11:5, Genesis 6:11–22). It is often thought that Enoch represents the Church, who will be taken to Heaven before the Tribulation, while Noah represents the faithful saints who will be preserved by God's grace during the Tribulation.

There is also the instance when Nebuchadnezzar, the king of the Babylonian Empire, told his officials to worship an idol of himself, or else they would be thrown into a fiery furnace (Daniel 3:1–7). Nebuchadnezzar could be seen here as a *type* or foreshadowing of the coming Antichrist, because the Antichrist will also force people to worship his Image, or they will be killed, as will be discussed more in later chapters.

The prophet Daniel's three friends were officials in the ancient Babylonian Empire, but they refused to worship Nebuchadnezzar's statue. As a result, they were thrown into a furnace that was heated to seven times as hot as normal (Daniel 3:19–23). This is also a foreshadowing of the seven-year Tribulation.

But God protected these three faithful men, so that when they stepped out of the furnace they were perfectly unharmed. Even their clothes did not smell like smoke (Daniel 3:27). This is like how God will miraculously protect his faithful saints during the Tribulation.

Where was Daniel during this incident? The Bible says that before the statue was created, Daniel was promoted to a high position that apparently made him exempt from being required to worship the statue (Daniel 2:48).

So Daniel is a foreshadowing of Christians who will be raptured (i.e., lifted up, caught up, raised up), to a "high position" (i.e., Heaven). They will not have to face the Tribulation, nor worry about not taking the Mark of the Beast and not worshipping the Image of the Beast.

In many other instances of divine judgment in the Old Testament, God either took his faithful people out of the way of the judgment, or God preserved them through the judgment. This is a clue to how God works, and it will happen again. God will rapture the

Church before the Tribulation, but God will also preserve his faithful saints who believe in him after the Rapture through the Tribulation.

All of this is strong evidence that the Rapture will indeed happen before the Tribulation.

Because people are told to watch for Jesus' return at the Rapture, it suggests that there will be specific signs that Christians will be able to see before the Rapture and Tribulation occur. The next chapter will look at these signs in more detail.

Before this, however, it is important to refute the claim that not all Christians will be raptured. It is only if all true Christians will be raptured that the Rapture could be a source of comfort and encouragement for Christians, instead of something that causes fear or anxiety.

WILL ALL CHRISTIANS BE RAPTURED?

Who will be raptured? Will it be all Christians, or only some Christians?

Sometimes it is said that only some portion of all the Christians who are living at the time of the Rapture will go to be with Jesus.

Usually, people who say this will argue that experiencing the Rapture is a reward for a Christian's faithfulness, or that the Rapture is only for Christians who are actively watching for Jesus' return.

Some legalists claim that Christians who are not worthy of being raptured will be left behind because they need to be purified from sin by enduring suffering during the Tribulation.

The Bible does hint that some Christians will not be "accounted worthy" of escaping everything that will happen in the Tribulation (Luke 21:36, KJV).

Other verses suggest that some Christians who are not paying attention to the signs will be caught off guard by Christ's sudden return (e.g., Revelation 3:3, 1 Thessalonians 5:3–6).

Some Christians might even be caught sinning against fellow Christians, which means that Jesus will be displeased with them (Matthew 24:45–51).

These verses, however, do *not* mean that these Christians will not be raptured!

Salvation is always on the basis of God's grace and personal faith in Jesus Christ, rather than good works (Ephesians 2:8–9, Romans 4:5, John 6:28–29).

Similarly, salvation from entering into the Tribulation will be on the basis of faith in Jesus, and not on the quality or quantity of Christians' good works, or how long someone has been a Christian, or anything else.

After all, it is clear that *all* deceased Christians who have truly trusted in Jesus as their Savior will be resurrected at the time of the Rapture (1 Thessalonians 4:16). Their resurrection does not depend on whether these Christians were watching for Jesus' return, or living holy enough lives when they died.

Similarly, 1 Thessalonians 4:17 does not include any hint that only some Christians who are alive at the Rapture will be caught up to be with Jesus.

More evidence that no Christian will be left behind at the Rapture comes from how there is no mention of the Church or churches anywhere in the Book of Revelation chapters 6 to 19. "Saints" are mentioned several times, because there will be many people who will believe in Jesus after the Rapture, but these new Christians will not be part of the Church.

This idea of there being some Christians who are not part of the Church may seem strange. However, it is similar to how although many faithful people believed in God and his promise of a coming Messiah during the Old Testament times, these people were also not part of the Church.

Dispensationalism is the idea that God works with different groups of people in different ways throughout different periods of history. These periods of time are called *dispensations*. Dispensationalism is a key part of many pre-Tribulation Rapture explanations.

There have been several dispensations throughout history. In every dispensation, the requirement for eternal salvation was always faith in God. Yet during these different dispensations, there have been different rules for how God wanted people to behave, or for how they should worship God. This is why Christians, as those who have believed in Jesus after his death and resurrection, no longer need to follow all of the Old Testament laws that God gave to the Israelites (Acts 15:6–11).

According to dispensationalists, the Church is a specific group of believers that began only at the first feast of Pentecost (also called the Feast of Weeks) after Jesus was resurrected. It was then that the Holy Spirit came to live inside these believers in a special way that did not occur for believers in the past (Acts 1:5, 2:1–4, 2:17–18).

Christians are now given the Holy Spirit to live in them the moment they first believe in Jesus, which unites them into the Church and guarantees their salvation (Ephesians 1:13–14, 4:30, Galatians 3:26–28, 1 Corinthians 6:17, 6:19, 2 Corinthians 1:21–22, Titus 3:5).

Evidence that the Church only includes people who will believe in Jesus from Pentecost up to the time of the Rapture comes from how Jesus said that the gates of hell will not overcome the Church (Matthew 16:18). Yet, during the Tribulation, the Antichrist *will* overcome the saints, and many of them will be killed for their faith (Revelation 13:7, 20:4).

Therefore, the saints who will live during the Tribulation are not the same group of people as the

Church, although both groups include Christians who believe in Jesus as their Savior.

There is further evidence to confirm this distinction between the Church and the saints who will live during the Tribulation.

Due to the special indwelling of the Holy Spirit mentioned earlier, all individual Christians who believed in Jesus from the time of Pentecost until the Rapture are part of the Church, which is in some spiritual sense, Christ's body (1 Corinthians 12:12-13, 12:27, Romans 12:4-6, Colossians 1:18, 1:24). This is still true for individual Christians who are living especially sinfully, and is also still true for Christians who are not watching for Jesus' return at the Rapture.

Yet there is no need for part of Christ's body to be punished or tortured again because of sin, because Christ suffered and died only once for all sin (1 Peter 3:18, Hebrews 7:27, 9:25-26, 1 John 2:2).

Christians who are baptized into Christ by having faith in him are considered to have died with Christ (Romans 6:3-5, 6:8-11). Therefore, Christ's perfect righteousness is given to Christians who put their faith in him (2 Corinthians 5:21, Romans 3:22-25, 1 Corinthians 1:30). As a result, there is no need for God to purify the Church by making some of its members suffer through the Tribulation because of their personal sins.

After all, no Christian is ever perfect in this life, and no Christian can say that he or she is not a sinner (1 John 1:8–10). Jesus instructed all Christians to pray for forgiveness (Matthew 6:12, Luke 11:4), which implies there will never be a time in a Christian's life that this prayer will be unnecessary.

While being part of Christ's body, the Church is also called the Bride of Christ (Ephesians 5:23, 5:31–32, Revelation 21:2, 21:9, 22:17). This is similar to how Eve was Adam's wife, and she was taken out of Adam's body, in particular, from Adam's rib (Genesis 2:20–24). Jesus was pierced by the soldier's spear in his side, out of which came blood and water (John 19:34). These symbolize the two sacraments of the Church: communion and baptism.

Therefore, because Christ loves his Church as his bride, and the Church is, in some spiritual sense, his own body, he will not leave part of his Bride behind to face God's wrath during the Tribulation (Ephesians 5:28–30).

In fact, it is possible to argue that the Church is seen in Heaven in Revelation chapter 4, right after John is told to "come up here," in a preview of the Rapture (Revelation 4:1–2).

In John's vision, the first thing he sees in Heaven is God's throne. The throne is surrounded by twenty-four other thrones. The "elders" who are seated on these thrones are wearing white robes and have golden crowns (Revelation 4:2–11). Angels are never described in the Bible as wearing crowns. So, since the only two types of intelligent beings that God has created are angels and humans, then these elders must be humans. But who are they?

Christians are promised that if they remain faithful during their lives, they will receive crowns, and will rule and reign with Christ as both kings and priests (2 Timothy 2:11–13, 1 Peter 2:9, Revelation 1:5–6, 2:10, 2:26–27, 3:11, 3:21, 5:9–10).

Christians' lives will also be judged by God after the Rapture, and Christians will receive greater or lesser amounts of eternal rewards and positions of authority in Jesus' eternal Kingdom on the basis of the good things they did during their lives (1 Corinthians 3:11–15, Luke 19:17).

Thus, these elders in John's vision most likely represent the resurrected, raptured, and glorified Christians who will be caught up to Heaven, judged, and rewarded before the Tribulation begins. This would be consistent with how Peter said that judgment will begin with the household of God (1 Peter 4:17), referring to Christians, before God will move on to judging the rest of the world during the Tribulation.

Note also that in the parable of the ten virgins (Matthew 25:1–13), which is often used to support a Mid-Tribulation or Post-Tribulation Rapture, there is no bride mentioned—only the bridegroom, and the virgins, who are called bridesmaids in some Bible translations.

So the virgins in this parable are better understood as referring to those saints who will put their faith in Jesus during the Tribulation. Only those saints who will endure by not giving up on their faith in Jesus throughout the Tribulation, despite facing severe persecution, will have their lives physically saved through the Tribulation (Matthew 24:13, Revelation 13:10, 14:12). These saints will get to celebrate at the Marriage Supper of the Lamb with Jesus and his bride, the Church, in Jesus's Millennial Kingdom. More will be said about this in chapter 8.

Another argument for the pre-Tribulation Rapture involves the "restrainer" who holds back the appearing of the Antichrist (2 Thessalonians 2:7–8). Many commentators identify the restrainer as the Holy Spirit, who indwells all true Christian members of the Church, which then lets the Church act as spiritual "salt" and "light" in the world (Matthew 5:13–16).

Salt was used in ancient times as a preservative to keep meat from rotting. So the influence of many spiritually-mature Christians within a society should help keep that society from falling into moral decay as quickly as it otherwise would.

Furthermore, Jesus is the light of the world, and light overcomes darkness (John 8:12). By extension, churches can be seen as lampstands that shine Jesus out into the world to hold back the spiritual darkness (Luke 8:16, Revelation 1:20).

But once the Rapture occurs and the Church is removed from the world, then the Holy Spirit will no longer operate as the Restrainer through the Church. This will allow the full power of Satan to be released on the world, and the Antichrist will be revealed to the world (2 Thessalonians 2:8–10). The appearance of the Antichrist on the world scene, backed up with Satan's power, is the very first judgment that begins the Tribulation (Revelation 6:1–2). Thus, the Church must be removed before the Antichrist can make his appearance.

Therefore, there are many Biblically-sound arguments to support the idea that all true Christians who are alive before the Rapture do not have to worry about experiencing the Tribulation, because the Rapture will happen before Jesus initiates the very first judgment described in the Book of Revelation.

This means that when Christians see all the signs of the end times beginning to occur, Christians can excitedly look up with anticipation for the Rapture, because their bodily redemption and heavenly reunion with Jesus is drawing near (Luke 21:28).

Chapter 3

Signs of the End Times

Jesus advised people to be watching for the signs of his return. Yet Jesus also said that he will come back when most people are not expecting it, like how a thief breaks into a house at night, when people are not on the lookout for him (Matthew 24:42–51, Luke 12:35–48, 2 Peter 3:10, Revelation 3:3, 16:15).

Jesus also said that the end times will come upon the world suddenly, like when a person walks into a trap or a snare (Luke 21:34–35). He warned that no one will know the exact day or hour of his return (Matthew 24:36, Mark 13:32).

Yet in 1 Thessalonians 5:1–11, the Apostle Paul gave additional details. He said that there will be two key traits of the coming end-times Tribulation that initially appear contradictory:

1. Most people will not see the Tribulation approaching.
2. Christians who are aware of what is happening in the world will be able to see the Tribulation approaching.

The reasons for this paradox will be explained in the rest of this chapter. This chapter will also discuss the signs that Christians should be able to watch for in order to know that Jesus' return at the Rapture will happen soon.

JESUS WILL RETURN UNEXPECTEDLY WHEN LIFE SEEMS "NORMAL" FOR MOST PEOPLE

Jesus warned that the next time he comes, the world will be similar to how it was in the days of Noah and Lot.

Noah lived thousands of years ago, before God judged the world for its wickedness by sending the worldwide Flood. The only people who survived were Noah, his wife, his three sons, and their wives.

God told Noah to build a large wooden boat and to stock it with food so that when the Flood suddenly came, Noah and his family would be saved. Noah took along on the Ark at least two of every animal that God sent to him, in order to repopulate the world after the Flood (Genesis chapters 6 to 8, Hebrews 11:7).

Much later, after the Flood, God warned Abraham that God would destroy the cities of Sodom and Gomorrah for their inhabitants' awful sins (Genesis 18:16–32). Yet Abraham's nephew Lot had ended up living in the city of Sodom, along with Lot's wife and daughters.

Angels had to persuade Lot and his wife and daughters to flee the city before it was suddenly destroyed. Lot's sons-in-law refused to leave, however, because they thought that Lot's warning about the imminent divine judgment was only a joke (Genesis 19:12–14).

Jesus used these two historical examples to warn that the next time he comes, it will also be at a time when life is continuing mostly as normal around the world. Most people will not be paying attention to any warnings about the coming divine judgments.

Regular daily activities like buying, selling, eating, drinking, marrying, building, and planting will be going on, just like in Noah's time and Lot's time before divine judgment suddenly came (Matthew 24:38–39, Luke 17:26–30).

People will even mock and scoff at the idea that Jesus is coming back soon, because they expect that life will continue to go on just like it always has (2 Peter 3:3–4, Jude 18). The scoffers will say this because they deliberately overlook times in the past when God judged the world for its sin, such as the worldwide Flood (2 Peter 3:5–7).

Yet these scoffers will be proven wrong in an awful way when the Rapture happens and God's end-times judgment suddenly begins. Once people see the events in the Book of Revelation beginning to be fulfilled, there will be no more scoffers who could reasonably deny that the end times have come (Revelation 6:15–17).

Also, just like in the worldwide Flood, Jesus warned that the Tribulation will be so terrible that if he did not shorten the days, no one would survive it (Mark 13:19–20, Matthew 24:21–22).

So, after all of the divine judgments and disasters that will happen during the Tribulation, it is very difficult to imagine that any of these descriptions of life continuing to go on normally for most of the world will be true at Jesus' Second Coming.

There is even a point in the Book of Revelation before Jesus' Second Coming where it describes God's judgment of something that is called "Babylon," which will be destroyed in a single hour (Revelation 18:9–10). This "Babylon" is not to be confused with the ancient city of Babylon that is now in the country of Iraq, or with the ancient Babylonian Empire.

There is debate among Bible prophecy experts over what "Babylon" represents in the Book of Revelation. Is it only a particular city? A specific country? The whole world? A false religion? Maybe "Babylon" will somehow be all of these things at once, like how, at the time when John wrote the Book of Revelation, Rome was both a city and an empire that covered most of the known world. Rome also had its own religion of emperor worship that was used to persecute Christians.

Prophecy experts today tend to argue that "Babylon" in the Book of Revelation is probably either one of two things: the left-behind remnants of the Roman Catholic Church after the Rapture, or the United States of America. More will be said on this topic later in this book.

Regardless of what "Babylon" actually is, after its destruction, the merchants of the world will mourn, because no one will be able to buy their luxury merchandise (Revelation 18:11–19). Then, there will also not be anyone playing music, working at the mill or as craftsmen, and no one will be getting married (Revelation 18:21–23). The destruction of "Babylon" will occur sometime before Jesus' Second Coming in Revelation chapter 19.

It seems to be clear that when Jesus returns at his Second Coming, everyday activities will *not* be going on for large portions of the world, because of how *all* the world's rulers, merchants, and shipmasters will be affected by Babylon's destruction (Revelation 18:9, 18:15, and 18:17–18).

Therefore, it is only during the time before the Rapture that Jesus would tell his followers to watch for his coming when life seems to be going on normally.

The Timing of Jesus' Second Coming

Furthermore, when Jesus said that no one knows the day or hour of his return (Matthew 24:36, Mark 13:32), he must also have been referring to the Rapture.

This is because it will be relatively easy for the people who will be on Earth during the Tribulation to figure out when Jesus' Second Coming will occur.

There are certain timelines given in the Bible that reveal exactly how long the Tribulation will last. Once specific events occur, people should be able to calculate the exact day of Jesus' Second Coming.

Daniel prophesied that Israel will sign a covenant with the Antichrist and "many." This covenant will be designed to last for a period of seven years, using the Babylonian calendar of 360 days per year (Daniel 9:27).

As will be discussed later in this book, it is the signing of this covenant that will officially begin the Tribulation period. Once this covenant is signed, people will be able to begin counting the days until the Tribulation will be over.

Additionally, there will be two notable individuals who will appear early on during the Tribulation, who the Bible calls the *Two Witnesses*. They will act very much like the Old-Testament prophets, who spoke God's word to the people and called on people to repent from their sins.

The Two Witnesses will prophesy in Jerusalem for the first 1,260 days of the Tribulation (Revelation 11:3). Using an average of thirty days in a month, that makes forty-two months, or three-and-a-half years.

During the time they are prophesying, the Two Witnesses will be able to miraculously cause droughts, turn water into blood, or cause plagues to happen (Revelation 11:3–6). The Two Witnesses will have miraculous powers to destroy anyone who threatens them, except for the Antichrist, who will kill them (Revelation 11:7).

This will probably occur at the mid-point of the Tribulation, when the Antichrist will enter the rebuilt Temple in Jerusalem and declare himself to be God (2 Thessalonians 2:3–4). The Two Witnesses will presumably call the Antichrist out on his lie, and so he will need to silence them.

The Antichrist will then rule over the world for another forty-two months, which is another 1,260 days, or three-and-a-half years, using an average of thirty days per month (Revelation 13:5, Daniel 12:11). At the end of this time, Jesus will return with the armies of

Heaven and defeat the Antichrist at the Battle of Armageddon (Revelation 19:11–21).

These events lay out a very clear timeline for Jesus' Second Coming at the end of the Tribulation. Jesus will return exactly 2,520 days after the Antichrist signs the covenant between Israel and "many."

Therefore, it is only when Jesus will return for the Rapture that the world could be caught by surprise, and will not know the exact day of his return.

Summary of the Differences Between the Rapture and Jesus' Second Coming

Based on all the previous discussion and supporting verses, it is clear that the Bible teaches that there are two different times when Jesus will return in the future, when the world will be in two very different situations.

First, at the Rapture, Jesus will come like a thief; unexpectedly and suddenly, at a day and hour that no one can predict.

Life will be going on normally, and people will deny that Jesus is coming soon, until Christians are transformed from mortal to immortal faster than the blink of an eye, and are suddenly caught up to meet Jesus in the clouds (1 Thessalonians 4:13–17, 1 Corinthians 15:50–54).

From there, raptured Christians will go to be with Jesus in Heaven, so that they will be spared from the Tribulation that will begin on Earth (John 14:1–3, Revelation 3:10).

The Rapture will catch the world off guard, and sudden destruction will come on the world as the Tribulation begins (1 Thessalonians 5:2–3).

Later, at Jesus' Second Coming, after the twenty-one unique divine judgments that are described in the Book of Revelation chapters 6 to 18, the world will have been through the worst period of suffering and disasters that it has ever experienced (Matthew 24:21–22).

At least a quarter of the world's population will have died from just the first four divine judgments (Revelation 6:8). The very last few judgments will make the world almost uninhabitable, and the final earthquake will flatten all cities (Revelation 16:3–4, 16:17–21).

At Jesus' Second Coming, every person in the world will see Jesus appear in the sky with his heavenly armies, and the whole world will mourn (Revelation 1:7, 19:11–16, Jude 14–15).

Therefore, when Jesus tells Christians to watch for his coming that will be like a thief breaking into a house, he is referring to the Rapture.

But how could Jesus expect Christians to be able to watch for his coming, if no one knows the day or hour of his return, and if the world will be going on normally?

How will Christians not be surprised by the Rapture, even though the rest of the world will walk into the Tribulation like when someone unexpectedly steps into a trap?

Jesus answered these questions by explaining that there will be certain signs that will indicate his return at the Rapture is coming soon.

Signs That Jesus Is Coming Back Soon For the Rapture

There are several different signs that the Bible says will indicate that the time when Jesus will return to take all real Christians to Heaven will be coming soon.

The first sign that Jesus said to look for was the rise of deception. Specifically, this warning was about people who will falsely claim to be Jesus, or say that they are God's true Messiah/Christ (Matthew 24:5, Luke 21:8). There will also be false prophets who will lead people astray by teaching false things about God (Matthew 24:11, 2 Peter 2:1, 1 Timothy 4:1-3).

Ultimately, this prophecy will be fulfilled by the man who is called the Antichrist, who will claim to be God (2 Thessalonians 2:3-4). The False Prophet will endorse the Antichrist's claims and help with his deception (Revelation 13:11-17).

Jesus also said that there will be wars and rumors of wars. These wars will be between kingdoms, but also between groups of people, as designated by the use of the Greek word *ethnos* (Matthew 24:6, Luke 21:9–10). So, the world will see wars between countries and also other sorts of conflicts or violence between different ethnic people groups. Some of these wars will turn into real conflicts, while others will just be "rumors" or looming threats of war.

Two of the largest wars in history were World Wars I and II. The Cold War could also be seen as a major "rumor" of war that never actually broke out, even though it was extremely close to doing so at some points. The world has also seen a number of recent conflicts between different ethnic groups of people who tried to eliminate one another.

More signs of the approaching end times include that there will be famines, earthquakes, and pestilences (i.e., diseases) in various places (Matthew 24:7, Luke 21:11).

Some Bible prophecy experts appeal to statistical analyses to claim that both famines and earthquakes are becoming more frequent and more severe. It should be obvious to everyone that the spread of disease is also now a major concern in the world.

There will also be other signs in the Sun, Moon, and stars (Luke 21:25). The Bible tells us that God made the Sun, Moon, and stars for the purpose of marking certain seasons, and to provide signs to humanity on certain days (Genesis 1:14–15). For example, there is a Christian documentary titled *The Star of Bethlehem*. In it, the producer Rick Larson used astronomical software to explore the celestial signs that may have occurred around the time of Jesus' birth, as well as at the time of Jesus' crucifixion.

Because of how Luke 21:25 mentions signs in the Sun, Moon, and stars, some Bible prophecy experts pay close attention to astronomical phenomena. In particular, there has been much interest in things like solar eclipses, lunar eclipses, and tetrads of blood moons that take place on particular days related to Old Testament feasts.

Usually, these prophecy experts argue that signs point to a particular time for either the Rapture, the Tribulation, or Jesus' Second Coming. For example, some experts emphasized the "Revelation 12" sign that occurred in 2017 as having some significance for end-times events, but it does not seem that much came from this supposed sign.

Some prophecy experts also point to the increase of things like solar flares, planetary alignments, near-misses of Earth by asteroids, and unusual meteors or meteorite activity as showing that the end times are near.

Signs in the sky could even include the strange unidentified flying objects (UFOs) that some pilots report seeing, and that governments claim to be studying.

UFOs are a particularly interesting sign of the end times, because secular governments around the world will need some sort of false explanation for the Rapture. A purported alien abduction of millions of people would probably be one of the most widely-accepted false explanations for the Rapture.

Western societies have already been set up for such a deception by generations of science-fiction books, radio programs, documentaries, and movies about aliens coming to Earth. Lately, governments are becoming more open to considering the possibility that aliens are the cause of some UFOs, as pilots and others send in reports of seeing unexplained activity in the skies or on radar sensors.

A few Christian researchers persuasively argue that people who see UFOs and people who claim to have had contact with aliens are being deceived, because it is only demons masquerading as aliens.

The purpose of this deceptive demonic activity would be to convince the world that aliens truly exist. The existence of aliens would imply that life on Earth is not specially created by God, but instead it evolved, just like how some scientists claim that alien life could have evolved on other planets.

This lie that the Rapture was a mass alien abduction might even appear to endorse the idea that aliens were the creators of humanity, rather than God. Some conspiracy theorists believe that such an idea is proven by their analysis of documents and relics that belonged to ancient pagan societies.

But the Bible is all about God's relationship to humans, who were specially created in the image of God (Genesis 1:26). Humanity is not an accident of nature, and humans did not evolve over millions of years from lesser life-forms.

Many scientists who are Christians that endorse creationism and intelligent design make strong cases for interpreting a wide variety of scientific evidence in a way that suggests the Earth is less than 10,000 years old. Various Christians in the past have argued this is true based on adding up the ages of people listed in the Bible's genealogies that go all the way back to Adam and Eve.

If the world really was created so recently, then evolution is impossible, because there would be simply not enough time for it to have occurred. Creationists thus provide alternative explanations for the scientific observations that evolutionists interpret as endorsing a much-older universe, such as tree rings, light from distant galaxies, and the layers of sediment in rocks around the world.

Creationists also point out major flaws with the theory of evolution, which even some non-Christian scientists are now beginning to slowly and quietly reject, because of these unresolved problems.

The Bible teaches that it was only because of Adam's sin that all creation was cursed to suffer decay and unproductivity, until it will be set free by God at some point in the future (Genesis 3:17-19, Romans 8:20-23). Yet if an intelligent alien species actually existed, it would not be fair for God to subject these aliens to a cursed and decaying universe only because humans sinned.

Furthermore, the Son of God became a human man named Jesus, in order to redeem all people who are descended from Adam and Eve—that is, all humans (Romans 5:12-19, Hebrews 2:14-17). Aliens or any other intelligent non-human species would thus be unredeemable, because they would not be biologically related to Adam and Eve, or to Jesus. This point will be returned to in Chapter 7, as it may answer the question of why anyone who takes the Mark of the Beast will be unable to be forgiven for this sin (Revelation 14:9-11).

In summary, there is no way to consistently fit another intelligent species into the Biblical narrative, except for angels. Angels are purely spiritual beings that were created by God to be ministers to humanity (Hebrews 1:13-14).

However, at some point in the past, a high-ranking angel named Lucifer became the devil when he chose to rebel against God (Ezekiel 28:11–19, Isaiah 14:12–15). One third of the angels sided with him, and they became fallen angels, also known as *demons* (Revelation 12:4–12).

The devil is now also called Satan, which in Hebrew means *the adversary* or *the enemy*. However, Satan can still disguise himself as an angel of light (2 Corinthians 11:14). He can also take on many other forms and shapes, like how he appeared to Eve in the Garden of Eden in the form of a serpent (Genesis 3:1–15, Revelation 12:9, 20:2). So, posing as aliens would not seem to be something that is difficult for Satan or his fallen angels to do.

Satan and his demons will be cast out of Heaven completely at some point in the future (Revelation 12:7–12). Eventually, they will be thrown into the Lake of Fire (Matthew 25:41, Revelation 20:14–15). But in the meantime, Satan and his demons cause trouble in the world and deceive people, in the hope of leading people to eternal destruction (1 Peter 5:8, John 8:44, 2 Corinthians 4:4).

Therefore, if Satan and his fallen angels could deceive many people into believing that aliens actually exist, not only would it undermine a Biblical worldview, but it would also provide a convenient set-up for the Antichrist to explain away the Rapture once it happens.

Whatever the lie will be about why Christians all around the world have suddenly disappeared, it will likely portray raptured Christians in a negative light. The Bible says the Antichrist will blaspheme or slander not only God, but also those who dwell/live in Heaven (Revelation 13:6). Raptured Christians would fit that description perfectly.

Such negative talk about raptured Christians would also help set up the world to accept the massive persecution of those people who will believe in Christ after the Rapture, as shown in the fifth judgment of the Tribulation (Revelation 6:9–11). This negativity toward Christians would also likely gain the world's support for the Antichrist's later war against the saints (Revelation 13:7).

This lie that the Rapture was actually an alien abduction might even be part of the great delusion that God says he will send on those people who reject the truth during the end times (2 Thessalonians 2:11–12). If this suggestion is correct, then Christians should watch for the topic of aliens and UFOs to become more accepted in society as the Rapture and Tribulation approach.

The last major sign of the end times is that people will become increasingly sinful and wicked, just like people were during the days of Noah and Lot (Genesis 6:5, 19:1–13, Matthew 24:38–39, Luke 17:26–30).

Paul provided several lists of traits that describe what people will be like in the end times (2 Timothy 3:1–5, Romans 1:28–32). A few of these traits include people being proud, disobedient, ungrateful, slanderous, lacking self-control, brutal, murderous, deceitful, envious, malicious, and loving money and themselves rather than God.

People will also reject the truth that they know about God, and instead worship nature. As punishment, God will allow them to become sexually immoral in many ways (Romans 1:18–27). People will even say that what is evil is good, and that what is good is actually evil (Isaiah 5:20). They will also encourage others to do things that are evil (Romans 1:32).

These are just some of the signs that the Bible says will indicate that the Rapture and the Tribulation are approaching.

Because the Rapture will happen before the Tribulation begins, other signs to watch for will include hints of things that will only happen during the Tribulation itself. For example, any signs that world events are leading toward the first four judgments in Revelation chapter 6 would be relevant.

Christians could also watch for signs of the formation of a world government with ten leaders, and a world religion that is opposed to the true teachings of

Christianity, because both of these things will exist during the Tribulation.

Any technology that leads toward enabling the Mark of the Beast that will control all buying and selling worldwide is also useful to watch for. The same goes for artificial intelligence or robotics technology that might enable the Image of the Beast that will be able to speak (Revelation 13:14–18).

Yet, it is not just these signs themselves, but also how often these signs occur, and how intense the signs are that offer important clues to the timing of Jesus' return at the Rapture.

THE SIGNS WILL INCREASE IN FREQUENCY AND INTENSITY

Jesus used the analogy of a pregnant woman's "birth pains" (i.e., labor contractions) to describe how all of these signs would start slowly, but increase in both frequency and intensity as the time for the Rapture approaches (Matthew 24:7–8, Mark 13:8).

Jesus also used the analogy of how ancient people in Israel could look at fig trees that put out leaves in the spring as a sign that summer is near. So Jesus said that when all of these signs are seen at the same time, it shows his return is very near. In fact, the generation who sees *all* of these things occurring will not completely die out before Jesus' Second Coming will happen (Matthew 24:32–34, Luke 21:29–32).

As Christians pay attention and see all of these signs occurring at the same time, and also increasing in frequency and intensity, they should know that Jesus' return at the Rapture is coming very soon (Luke 21:28).

However, to everyone else, it will seem that the world is just going through a rough time, as has happened in the past. Most people will not seem to be overly concerned, and they will scoff when Christians point out these signs that indicate the nearness of Jesus' return (2 Peter 3:3–4).

But it is not just these specific signs that Christians should look for, because as many scoffers correctly say, these things have always been happening, and yet life goes on. Therefore, two additional clues are necessary to identify the approximate time period when Jesus will appear for the Rapture.

These clues are:

1. What the Bible says many churches will be like in the last days.
2. The re-establishment of the state of Israel, in the same land that it historically occupied in the Middle East.

Both of these signs will be discussed in the rest of this chapter.

The Condition of the Church in the Last Days

As the world becomes more sinful, Christians will feel increasingly frustrated by what they see happening, just like how Lot was disturbed by the sin that went on around him in Sodom (2 Peter 2:7–8).

Christians will also be persecuted by these evil people who will become morally worse and more deceptive (2 Timothy 3:12–13).

Many Christians will even fall away from their faith, and will betray each other because of persecution (Matthew 24:9–10). Jesus warned these Christians that there will be negative consequences for their mistreatment of fellow Christians (Matthew 24:48–51).

However, although persecution of Christians will increase as the end times approach, there is a clue that Christianity as a whole will not be completely outlawed before the Rapture.

Thus, most churches will not have to return to operating in secret, like they did during some times in the past, or in some areas of the world today where Christianity is severely persecuted.

This argument relies on what the Bible suggests most Christian churches will be like in the last days before the Rapture. This theory is somewhat speculative, but it seems historically plausible.

This theory is based on the idea that the seven churches in Revelation chapters 2 and 3 were not just seven particular churches that existed in what is now the country of Turkey. Instead, it is argued that these seven churches, despite being very real churches with particular problems, also prophetically reveal the history of the (mostly Western) Church, from the time of the early church, until the Rapture.

In this theory:

The church in Ephesus represents the early church that began in Jerusalem at the first Pentecost after Jesus's resurrection, and then grew as Christianity spread outward to several major cities around the eastern Roman Empire (Revelation 2:1–7). These early Christians were occasionally persecuted, and successfully weeded out false teachers. But as a whole, the early church slowly lost the passionate love that it originally had for Jesus.

The church in Smyrna represents the persecuted church in the second and third centuries AD (Revelation 2:8–11). At that time, many Roman emperors and governors tortured and killed Christians during several different periods of persecution, some of which were limited to particular regions or cities.

The church in Pergamum represents the church after Christianity was legalized by Emperor Constantine in 313 AD (Revelation 2:12–17). Christians began to gain wealth, status, and influence in the Roman Empire. Several church councils successfully overcame some heresies about Jesus that had appeared and were gaining popularity.

But the Roman church during this time also brought in a non-Biblical hierarchical power structure that raised up the clergy over the laity. A few non-Biblical practices also began to creep into Christian spirituality and worship.

The church in Thyatira represents the church of the Middle Ages (Revelation 2:18–29). During this time, theologians in the Western church tended to raise up the value of Aristotelian philosophy and used it to interpret Christianity, which led to some theological distortions.

Less focus was placed on teaching the gospel to the common people, who were forbidden from owning copies of the Bible or hearing church services in their own native languages. Church leaders often became more concerned about achieving political power or wealth, and immorality increased among the clergy.

During this era, there were also further non-Biblical rituals and spiritual practices incorporated into the Western church. Yet some people in the church still truly loved God and did their best to help others in need.

The church in Sardis represents the church during the Reformation that began in the early 1500s (Revelation 3:1–6). It was then that Martin Luther and other

Reformers began to point out problems in the Roman Catholic Church's theology and spiritual practices. Eventually, the Reformers founded their own churches that rejected many of what they saw as the most blatant errors that had crept into the Roman Catholic Church.

Yet these new Protestant churches often became state-sponsored churches. Many European governments soon forced all of their citizens to attend these churches and be baptized, even though some of these church members did not have personal faith in Christ. This action turned attending church services into an expected cultural activity that made it a meaningless ritual for many people, when it should have been a vibrant worship gathering of faithful believers in Jesus.

Today, many of these traditional Protestant denominations that were founded at that time are in decline. Their congregations are aging, and they are unable to attract or retain enough new members to replace members who die. These denominations are also being tempted to endorse, or at least tolerate, specific sins that are now popular in Western culture, which drives those Christians who want to uphold biblical morality away from these churches.

The church in Philadelphia represents the churches that were behind the worldwide missionary movement and spiritual revivals that began in the seventeenth and eighteenth centuries (Revelation 3:7–13).

These churches and movements were focused on teaching that people needed to truly believe in Jesus for eternal salvation, instead of trusting in religious rituals like baptism or communion, or relying on the authority of the state-sponsored churches. Christians in these churches often faced opposition and persecution from the state-sponsored churches, and this led many of them to leave Europe in search of safety in North America.

Today, all churches that preach the true gospel of eternal salvation by faith alone in Christ alone, without relying in any way on good works, and that encourage people to have a real relationship with Jesus can be considered as being part of the church of Philadelphia.

The last "church" of Laodicea represents what large parts of "Christianity" will be like in the last days just before the Tribulation begins (Revelation 3:14–22). Jesus said that this church appears to be outwardly wealthy and successful, but actually it is spiritually poor, blind, naked, and pitiful.

Jesus is also disgusted by this church, because it does not provide either spiritual refreshment or medicinal warmth to its surrounding society (Revelation 3:15–16). He warns people in this church that they need to come to him to gain true spiritual riches, to be spiritually clothed in Christ's righteousness by having their sins forgiven (e.g., Galatians 3:27, Romans 13:14), to have their eyes spiritually opened to the truth, and to enter into a loving personal relationship with Jesus, through having faith in him.

Metaphorically, Jesus is on the outside of this church and is knocking to see if anyone will let him into their hearts. This implies that many people who attend this "church" are not true Christians, even if they appear to put on a good show.

There have always been people who believed that they were Christian, and who attended and participated in church activities, but who had never actually personally trusted in Jesus Christ as their Savior. Paul warned that during the end times, many more people like this will appear.

They will appear to be righteous, and they might even say the right things, but their lives will show that they have not experienced the real power of the gospel message (2 Timothy 3:5).

Jesus warned that at the Final Judgment, these people will claim to have served him and to have done all sorts of good works for him. However, Jesus will know that they never really believed in him, and so they will not have eternal life (Matthew 7:21–23). They are people who think they can earn their salvation through good works, rather than simply trusting in God's free grace by having faith in Jesus (Romans 3:21–28, John 3:16).

These people will be left behind at the Rapture, but they will likely still call themselves Christians. These people, if they do not realize that they never truly believed in Jesus, might become part of "Babylon," which could possibly be a pseudo-Christian religion that will persecute true Christians (Revelation 6:9–11, 17:6, 18:4).

These false Christians who will be left behind may also attempt to convince others that the Rapture has not actually occurred. They will say they are Christians, and so if it was really the Rapture, then they should have been taken also. Therefore, they will say that it must have been something else, such as an alien abduction, or whatever the authorities will claim it was.

Today, a number of end-times prophecy experts believe that the Laodicean "church" can represent many contemporary churches, including some mega churches.

The "church" of Laodicea would also include those churches that preach the prosperity gospel. This teaching claims that God wants to make all Christians rich, healthy, and successful in this life, in exchange for their donations to particular organizations or ministries. Yet Paul was clear that true Christianity is not about making people materially wealthy in this life (1 Timothy 6:5–10).

These Laodicean churches also "taste" about the same as their surrounding culture, thanks to how they try to incorporate music that is similar to what is heard on secular radio channels, but the songs usually have very little theological content. These churches also usually have casual dress codes, pastors with strong charisma, theatrical worship performances, and feel-good sermons in order to draw people into these churches.

Often, pastors in these churches do not even dare to preach about sin or the need for people to believe in Jesus to have eternal life. They worry that telling people they are sinners who are heading toward eternal death unless they repent by believing in Jesus will offend people and drive their audience away. Then the church will lose money, and the pastor will lose prestige and influence.

As a result, such churches can offer the world nothing different from what the culture already has, and so they are spiritually "lukewarm" (Revelation 3:16).

Therefore, it seems that the Church as a whole has now experienced each of the historical conditions that are laid out in Revelation chapters 2 and 3, as represented prophetically by these seven historical churches.

It should be noted that not every church in every time period was defined by the above descriptions. Yet, in general, it seems like this interpretation of the seven churches in Revelation is fairly historically accurate, if it is thought to represent which churches tended to have the most influence in society during these periods of time.

In particular, the last church of Laodicea seems to accurately describe the bland, watered-down "Christianity" that is found in many churches today. It is these churches that, as a whole, are currently some of the most culturally influential in the world, in terms of how many people follow their pastors on social media, how many people stream their services online, and how much their concerns and attitudes dominate the Christian music, book, and film industries.

This historical timeline of the Church also fits with how, immediately after John finished writing the letters to these churches, he saw a vision of a door standing open in Heaven, and a voice like a trumpet called him to "come up here" (Revelation 4:1). This description seems to fit well with what Paul wrote about the Rapture, which will involve Christians being suddenly caught up into Heaven at the sound of a trumpet and the voice of the archangel (1 Thessalonians 4:16–17).

Therefore, it seems that if these seven churches do represent a sort of timeline that describes the historical condition of the Church, then John's vision of being called up to Heaven in Revelation 4 would correspond with a pre-Tribulation Rapture that will occur before the first judgment of the Tribulation begins in Revelation 6.

This, then may be a clue that the Rapture will happen after the church of Laodicea has become the dominant condition of the Western church. If so, then it does not seem that the Church as a whole will revert to the persecuted state of the church of Smyrna before the Rapture happens.

Therefore, Christians should expect that as the end times approach, the culture-friendly "lukewarm" churches that water down the gospel will continue to maintain their popularity and positions of cultural influence. In contrast, the faithful evangelical churches will feel like they have only a little strength left (Revelation 3:8).

The Re-Establishment of Israel and Reconstruction of the Temple in Jerusalem

Finally, one of the most significant signs of the approaching end times is the re-establishment of the nation of Israel.

After all, Israel must exist in order for the Antichrist to sign a covenant between Israel and "many," which will trigger the beginning of the Tribulation period that lasts for approximately seven years (Daniel 9:27).

Furthermore, as will be discussed more in Chapter 8, there are several important purposes that God will achieve during the Tribulation. One of these purposes is to bring most of the people of Israel to the point where they will recognize that Jesus is their true Messiah. This is the necessary pre-condition for Jesus' Second Coming (Matthew 23:37–39, Zechariah 12:10–13).

If there were no one who was descended from Abraham, Isaac, and Jacob in the land of Israel who could say "Blessed is he who comes in the name of the Lord," then Jesus' prophecy in Matthew 23:37–39 could not be fulfilled, and Jesus would be unable to return to Earth.

So, theoretically, if Satan could prevent Israel from saying this and calling out for Christ to save them, then Satan could prevent Jesus' Second Coming from happening.

This fact explains why Satan has always attempted to persecute and destroy Israel and the Jewish people. Because Satan failed to stop Jesus' First Coming (Revelation 12:1–6), Satan's only hope to avoid being locked up in the supernatural jail of the "bottomless pit," and later on, avoid his eternal destruction in the Lake of Fire (Revelation 20:1–3, 20:10), would be for Satan to find some way to stop Jesus' Second Coming from happening.

Satan's final attempt to destroy Israel will happen at the Battle of Armageddon, at the very end of the Tribulation (Revelation 16:12–16). Once the remnant of Israel realizes that Jesus is their true Messiah and cries out for him to save them from total annihilation, Jesus will return. The Antichrist will then try to actually fight against Jesus and his armies, but will completely fail (Revelation 19:11–21).

Additionally, there must be a rebuilt Temple in Jerusalem in order for the Antichrist to declare himself to be God inside it (2 Thessalonians 2:3–4). When it is rebuilt, it will be the third Temple that Israel has ever had, as the previous two were destroyed in the past. Yet this third Temple could not exist without Israel once again existing and having control over the city of Jerusalem and the Temple Mount.

Today, there is growing interest among the people in Israel to see their Temple rebuilt. There are even groups in Israel who have been planning for the Temple's reconstruction by preparing all of the equipment and materials that will be necessary. This includes the Temple's furnishings, the utensils and bowls, the menorah, the altar, the priests' garments, and so forth.

It is possible that they may even have blueprints ready, so that as soon as there is political approval, the construction of the third Temple could be rapidly completed. There are also plans underway to construct a rail line from Tel Aviv to the Temple Mount, to make it easy for everyone who wants to worship there to travel to the third Temple.

Currently, there is debate among Bible prophecy experts about whether the Dome of the Rock could remain standing while the Temple is rebuilt. Some experts believe the Dome of the Rock will be destroyed in order to clear the way for the reconstruction of the third Temple. Other experts claim that the third Temple could be built near the Dome of the Rock, since there appears to be enough room for both structures to share the Temple Mount, as long as the outer courtyard of the Temple is not built (Revelation 11:1–2).

Another thing the priests will need for the Temple are the ashes of a perfectly red-colored heifer, which is a particular type of cow. One of these cows must reach a certain age without having more than one or two non-red hairs, and with no blemishes anywhere on it, in order for it to be qualified to be sacrificed (Numbers 19). Once the heifer is sacrificed and burned, its ashes can be used to purify the priests who will serve in the rebuilt Temple.

Prophecy experts have shown much interest in the progress toward breeding a pure red heifer. It seems that for the last decade or so, every few years, there has been talk of a potential cow that might meet these necessary criteria.

There also was some interest among prophecy experts in the 1980s in attempting to figure out where the Ark of the Covenant is currently located.

The Ark of the Covenant was constructed by the Israelites after they left Egypt. It contained the two stone tablets that the Ten Commandments were written on, as well as a few other important historical artifacts, and the Ark was a place of God's presence on Earth (Exodus 25:10–22).

The Ark would typically sit in the innermost part of the Tabernacle tent, and later, the Temple, where the High Priest would go only once a year to perform an important ritual on the Day of Atonement (Hebrews 9:1–7, Leviticus 16).

However, the Ark of the Covenant was never recorded as being captured during the Roman destruction of the second Temple in 70 AD. It is not clear what happened to it, or where it might now be located. Some prophecy experts have claimed that it would be necessary to find the Ark in order to properly restart the worship of God in the third Temple, by placing the Ark into the innermost room of the Temple that is called the Holy of Holies.

In the past decade, though, there has been much less focus on the Ark of the Covenant. Some prophecy experts seem to assume that the Israeli government has already found the Ark during excavations under the ruins of the Temple Mount, and so they are currently keeping the Ark in a top-secret location. Others say that perhaps God will reveal the location of the Ark only after the Temple is finally rebuilt, to allow the Ark to be relocated back into the Temple where it belongs.

Possibly, the Temple could be rebuilt without having the Ark of the Covenant in the Holy of Holies. This could be compatible with how some prophecy experts argue that rebuilding the Temple will actually be a sin, because God no longer wants to be worshiped in that manner, now that Jesus has come and inaugurated the New Covenant through his death on the cross (e.g., Hebrews 9:11–28, 10:1–18, Jeremiah 31:31–34, Luke 22:19–20). If so, then perhaps God *intended* for the Ark of the Covenant to be lost.

This argument could be supported by how after Jesus' death, the curtain in the second Temple that separated the people from the Holy of Holies was torn completely in half from top to bottom (Matthew 27:51, Mark 15:38).

This curtain was very thick, and the fact that it tore beginning from the top, without any human intervention, was a powerful divine message. It indicated that there was no longer any need for animal sacrifices to make people right with God, because Jesus himself was the final, perfect sacrifice for all sin (Hebrews 7:27, 9:24–28, 10:12). It also showed that people now have direct access to God through prayer, without needing human priests to mediate for them (Hebrews 4:15–16).

Therefore, any attempt to return to the system of Old Testament sacrifices without God's authorization would be an insult to God, because it would imply that Jesus' death was not good enough to pay for all sin. This mistake would be just as serious of a sin as when the religious leaders of Jesus' time rejected Jesus as their Messiah and wanted to kill him (Hebrews 6:4–6). Yet this argument will not convince anyone who does not accept that Jesus truly was the Messiah.

The main obstacle to rebuilding the third Temple is simply the political approval it would require. Currently, many other countries and groups in the Middle East are very concerned that Israel might try to destroy the Dome of the Rock or rebuild the Temple. Something will have to change dramatically in terms of international politics in order to make it feasible for Israel to rebuild their Temple without causing international outrage or sparking another war in the Middle East.

Perhaps the political situation will be altered and become favorable to rebuilding the Temple after the Psalm 83 War and/or Gog-Magog War (Ezekiel 38). These wars will be discussed more in the Appendix of this book. Or perhaps it will be the Antichrist's covenant that will allow Israel to rebuild the Temple while still having peace with Israel's neighbors (Daniel 9:27).

Some prophecy experts also look at the date of the re-establishment of the state of Israel on May 14, 1948, to be a major sign that the world is approaching the end times. This event was in itself a major fulfillment of Bible prophecy (e.g., Isaiah 66:8, Jeremiah 16:14–15, Ezekiel 37). In fact, this may be such an important sign that none of the other signs of the end times even mattered until Israel was re-established. The theological argument for this idea relies on a more detailed interpretation of Jesus' words about the fig tree in Matthew 24:32–34.

Instead of interpreting these verses as only saying that the generation of people who see all of these signs beginning to occur will also see Jesus' Second Coming, the fig tree can also be seen as a symbol of Israel. As a result, prophecy experts often argue that the same generation of people who saw the re-establishment of Israel will also see Jesus' Second Coming.

Evidence for this interpretation comes from how Jesus may have used the fig tree as a symbol for Israel, when he complained that he had hoped to find figs on the tree (i.e., faith in himself), but figs were not in season (Mark 11:12–14). Similarly, Jesus was rejected by the majority of the people alive at the time of his First Coming, and especially by most of the religious leaders. The symbol of figs being used to refer to the faithful or unfaithful people of Israel is also found in Jeremiah chapter 24.

If this is a plausible interpretation, then Jesus's comments about the generation that sees the fig tree produce leaves could indeed predict that at least some of the people of the generation which saw Israel become a recognized nation again in 1948 will still be alive at Jesus' Second Coming. If this is true, then this prophecy of the fig tree acts as a sort of upper limit on how many years can pass between the re-establishment of Israel and the end of the Tribulation.

However, it is not clear exactly how long a generation is. In the past, some prophecy experts thought it was only forty years, such as the generation of Israelites who wandered the wilderness for that length of time (Numbers 14:33). This idea led to some hype that Jesus would return in 1988, forty years after 1948, but it did not happen.

After that, some prophecy experts picked up on Psalm 90:10 that suggests a generation is seventy or eighty years long. If so, that would put the timeframe for Jesus' Second Coming between 2018 and 2028.

Yet as of the date of writing this book, it is 2023, and the seven-year Tribulation has not yet begun, since the pre-Tribulation Rapture has not yet occurred. So that means 2028 is too soon for Jesus' Second Coming.

So perhaps it is better not to identify a particular length of time that meets the definition of a generation. Instead, this prophecy could simply mean that at least some people who saw the re-establishment of Israel will be alive at Jesus' Second Coming, even if they are very old and not many of them are left alive.

This interpretation of this prophecy could still be fulfilled, because as of 2023, people born in 1948 are seventy-five years old. Although these people are becoming old, some of them could live for a couple more decades.

Many prophecy experts currently look to the date of 2033 as being significant for the end times, because it would be exactly two-thousand years from when Jesus was crucified and resurrected. This is within the approximate lifespans of some of these people who were born in 1948.

In summary, the re-establishment of the nation of Israel within the same historical boundaries, with the capital of Jerusalem, and which is gaining interest in constructing the third Temple are certainly important signs of the approaching Tribulation. When these signs are combined with all the others discussed in this chapter, it makes a very compelling argument that the Tribulation will begin very soon.

The fact that all these signs are occurring with greater frequency and intensity, and within the approximate time-span prophesied by Jesus using the analogy of the fig tree, should cause all Christians to wake up and pay attention, so that they are not found to be spiritually asleep when Jesus returns (Luke 12:37–38).

Christians can be ready for Jesus to return at any moment by sharing the gospel, and telling people about the coming Tribulation so that non-Christians can choose to believe in Jesus now, before the Rapture happens.

If people believe in Jesus before the Rapture, it will be much better for them than if they had to live on Earth during all the terrible things that will happen during the Tribulation. These events will be the focus of the next chapter.

Chapter 4

The Events of the Tribulation

The Rapture will be the event that moves the world from a time of relative normalcy to a time of chaos and divine judgment during the seven-year Tribulation.

However, some prophecy experts debate how soon the Tribulation will begin after the Rapture happens.

What Will Happen After The Rapture

Some experts believe that there will be a period of time between the Rapture and the beginning of the Tribulation.

This time would be necessary for the world to deal with the aftermath of the Rapture, and the societal chaos it would cause.

For example, if even ten percent of the population of the Western world suddenly disappeared, it would cause incredible disruption.

After the Rapture, Christians who worked in many different jobs will have been caught up to Heaven, and so it would take time for their former employers to replace them with others and train them. In the meantime, no one would have the knowledge or expertise to fulfill the roles or complete the tasks that need to be done in order for the world to run smoothly.

This will be especially true for Christians who were in critical roles in areas of government, emergency response, infrastructure operations, law enforcement, the military, health care, and any business or organization that relies on a top-down chain of command.

The Rapture will also likely leave many empty vehicles unattended on highways and streets. It will take time for tow trucks to clear these vehicles away, so that supplies can be delivered once again to where they need to go.

This will be a challenge because of how there will also be fewer tow truck drivers, other types of truck drivers, dispatchers, air-traffic control operators, and pilots, because some people in these occupations will also have been raptured.

However, some prophecy experts believe that the Tribulation will not officially begin until as late as the sixth judgment. This claim is made on the basis that the Book of Revelation records that it is only then that people will cry out because they recognize that the wrath of God is coming on the world (Revelation 6:15–17).

These experts also argue that the martyrs who die during the fifth judgment do not seem to know how much longer it will be before those who killed them are judged (Revelation 6:10). Yet, because the Tribulation will last exactly seven years, if it began in the very first judgment in Revelation 6:1–2, then it seems that the martyrs should know exactly how long it will be until Jesus will return and judge the world.

Those prophecy experts who support this perspective propose that the first five judgments in Revelation chapter 6 could occur during the gap after the Rapture, but before the official beginning of the seven-year Tribulation. These experts sometimes interpret the first judgment as some new world government rising to power, but not as the appearance of the Antichrist himself, nor the signing of the seven-year covenant between Israel and "many" (Daniel 9:27).

On the other hand, other prophecy experts argue that the chaos caused by the Rapture would be the perfect time for the Antichrist to rise to power. This claim corresponds well with how the Bible says that it is only the Holy Spirit, operating through the Church, who is the "restrainer" that prevents the Antichrist from being revealed (2 Thessalonians 2:3–10).

Therefore, the moment that all true believers in Jesus are raptured, the Holy Spirit will no longer prevent the Antichrist from making his debut on the world stage. Therefore, most Bible prophecy teachers identify the first judgment in Revelation 6:1–2 as the revealing of the Antichrist. There is good evidence for this interpretation which will be discussed later in this chapter.

If this interpretation is correct, the very first judgment would coincide with the official beginning of the Tribulation, because the Antichrist is identified by the covenant he will sign between Israel and many others (Daniel 9:27).

Furthermore, it seems unbelievable that the first four judgments could be interpreted as not being part of God's wrath, given that at least twenty-five percent of the world's population will die during these judgments (Revelation 6:8).

So perhaps the world simply will not realize that it is God's wrath until the sixth judgment. In the fifth judgment, the martyrs in Heaven who cry out to God could be interpreted not as asking a question because they don't know something, but as asking for God to quickly bring justice on their persecutors.

Regardless of how it occurs, there will likely be at least a few days between the Rapture and the official start of the Tribulation. It could also be as long as several months, or even a year or two, depending on how much needs to happen in order for everything in the world to be fully set up for the Tribulation to begin, such as perhaps the Psalm 83 War and Gog-Magog War (Ezekiel 38).

Yet it will most certainly not be decades between when the Rapture happens and when the judgments in Revelation chapter 6 begin.

The Seal Judgments

The Seal judgments are the first seven judgments, out of the total of twenty-one divine judgments that will occur during the Tribulation. These first seven judgments are symbolically depicted in the Book of Revelation as Jesus breaking open wax seals on a scroll, which only he is qualified to open (Revelation 5).

These seven Seal judgments will be followed by seven Trumpet judgments that are depicted as angels blowing trumpets. Finally, seven Bowl judgments are depicted as angels pouring out bowls of God's wrath onto the Earth.

The first four Seal judgments have some similarities, because all four are symbolically depicted as men who come riding out on horses, once the corresponding seal is opened by Jesus.

Some prophecy experts wonder why only these four judgments are depicted as horsemen. What is special about these judgments, in comparison to the other Seal judgments?

There is speculation by prophecy experts that perhaps these first four judgments are manmade disasters. Yet the symbolism of these judgments being represented as men riding out on horses might also simply represent how quickly the judgments will begin to occur, one after the other.

THE FIRST SEAL JUDGMENT (THE RIDER ON THE WHITE HORSE)

Revelation 6:1–2 says that the first rider appears on a white horse. Jesus will also ride a white horse when he will appear in the clouds to fight the Battle of Armageddon (Revelation 19:11). This similarity suggests that the first rider on the white horse is a false Christ, that is, the *Antichrist*.

In Western culture today, the image of a knight who comes riding in on a white horse is usually seen to represent a hero or savior figure. The same will likely be true of the Antichrist. He will seem to know exactly what to do to solve the chaos the world will be facing after the Rapture, and many people will be deceived into thinking that he is a hero or savior.

His deception will be enhanced by the "strong delusion" that God will send as a punishment on many left-behind people because they rejected the truth and enjoyed unrighteousness (2 Thessalonians 2:11–12, Romans 1:28).

When the first rider on the white horse appears on the world scene, the Bible says that he already has conquered in some way or another, and yet he still goes forth to conquer even more (Revelation 6:1–2). However, he does not seem to conquer by using violence, because although the rider has a bow, he is simply given a crown.

Some Bible prophecy experts debate what this rider's crown and bow represent.

The crown seems clear, as the Greek term *stephanos* simply means a crown, probably like the wreathes of leaves that were given to victors in ancient Greek and Roman athletic competitions. The symbol of the crown would make sense if the Antichrist has conquered or been victorious in some way. As a result of his victory, he has gained some position of authority in the world.

The symbol of the bow is more difficult, because this specific Greek word *toxon* is used only once in the entire Bible, in this verse.

In Greek, *toxon* can mean a weapon used in archery, and many artistic depictions of the four horsemen portray it this way. Some prophecy experts also note that because the first horseman does not have any arrows, this detail might also suggest that he conquers through peace or peacefully. However, *toxon* can also refer to anything arched, like a rainbow. Another meaning could be a thin piece of fabric, perhaps like a ribbon that a medal of achievement might hang from.

These symbols of the crown and bow will likely make complete sense to those people who are left behind after the Rapture, who will see the Antichrist come to power.

Daniel 8:23–25 gives a short description of the Antichrist's entire career. Here, some English Bible translations say that through masterful deception and peace, the Antichrist will "destroy many" people who were not expecting it (Daniel 8:25).

The Antichrist is also identified as the "man of lawlessness" (2 Thessalonians 2:3), suggesting that he will not follow laws, may break his agreements with others, or he may even change many laws (Daniel 7:25).

Bible prophecy experts teach that the Antichrist will be identifiable because he will negotiate, confirm, or strengthen some sort of covenant between Israel and "many" that is originally set to last for seven years (Daniel 9:27). It is often thought that this covenant will be a peace treaty between Israel and many of the surrounding nations that have been Israel's enemies at various times in history.

Likely, this covenant that will be confirmed or strengthened by the Antichrist will allow Israel to rebuild their Temple on the Temple Mount in

Jerusalem. Some experts associate this covenant with the "covenant of lies" that Israel will make with "death" and "Hell/Hades/Sheol" in Isaiah 28:14–18. However, the Antichrist will break this treaty three--and-a-half years later, in an event called the *Abomination of Desolation*, which will be discussed more in the next chapter.

Thus, there is strong evidence that the First Seal judgment that is represented by the coming out of the rider on the white horse is the appearance of the Antichrist. He will be identified by how he will be involved in the confirming, signing, or strengthening of some sort of peace deal between Israel and "many."

The signing of this peace treaty will fulfill Paul's prophecy that when the people of the world will be saying "peace and safety/security," then they will face sudden destruction (1 Thessalonians 5:2–3). This sudden destruction may begin during the Second Seal judgment, symbolized by the next horseman who rides out on a red horse.

THE SECOND SEAL JUDGMENT (THE RIDER ON THE RED HORSE)

The idea that the Antichrist will gain power peacefully is supported by how it is only during the Second Seal judgment that the world breaks out into violence and/or war (Revelation 6:3–4).

Prophecy experts often propose that the rider on the red horse, who appears when Jesus opens the second seal, could represent World War III. The "great sword" that the rider carries could be nuclear weapons. However, this judgment could also simply be an outbreak of many other sorts of local wars and violence all around the world, with the large sword representing how widespread or deadly the violence will be.

This judgment corresponds with how Jesus warned that one of the signs of the end times would be wars and rumors of wars (Matthew 24:6, Mark 13:7). These wars will be between different countries, but also between different ethnic groups of people. The original Greek text uses the word *basileia*, meaning "kingdoms," and *ethnos*, meaning "nations" or groups of people who share similar ethnic traits (Matthew 24:7).

Currently, it seems that there are many potential hot-spots where wars could break out around the world at almost any moment. Many of these wars could occur during the Second Seal judgment.

If nuclear weapons are used, though, they will not destroy the entire world, because Jesus said the Tribulation will end before everyone on the planet dies (Matthew 24:22, Mark 13:20). There are also still nineteen more judgments that are prophesied to occur during the Tribulation period, so the entire world will not end due to nuclear war or World War III in the Second Seal judgment.

THE THIRD SEAL JUDGMENT
(THE RIDER ON THE BLACK HORSE)

When Jesus opens the third seal, another rider comes out on a black horse. This rider is carrying a pair of balance scales, like what were used in ancient markets to calculate prices for goods.

The Third Seal is described as something that will cause the price of food to skyrocket, especially the price of wheat and barley (Revelation 6:5–6).

The average amount that a worker is paid each day (in Greek, this was called a *denarius*) will only be enough to buy a quart of wheat, or three quarts of barley. In today's terms, this could be like a loaf or two of bread.

But the rider is told not to harm the oil or the wine (Revelation 6:6). In the first century AD, oil and wine were luxury items that not everyone could afford. Perhaps this means that people who are rich enough will be relatively less affected by this judgment, and they will still able to afford luxuries.

It is not clear exactly what it will be that causes food prices to increase to such extremes during this judgment. Over the years, prophecy experts have suggested that it could be anything from a worldwide economic collapse worse than the Great Depression, hyperinflation, or a terrible worldwide famine.

The economic disturbance that will be caused by the disappearance of many farmers in the Rapture, and by the wars in the Second Seal judgment, may also contribute to the dramatic increase of food prices that will be seen in the Third Seal judgment.

The Fourth Seal Judgment (The Rider on the Pale Horse)

The rider who comes out on a pale horse during the Fourth Seal is named "Death," and he is followed by *Hades*, sometimes translated into English as "Hell" (Revelation 6:7–8).

In Greek mythology, *Hades* was the place of the dead, and also the name of the Greek god of the underworld. In the New Testament, the word *Hades* is used as a synonym for the Hebrew word *Sheol*, which means "grave" or "underworld" (Acts 2:27, Psalm 16:10). Sheol/Hades is described as a temporary place of storage for unsaved souls (Luke 16:23, Revelation 20:14).

In the Fourth Seal judgment, "Death" and "Hell" are given power over twenty-five percent of the world. People will die because of violence, starvation, pestilence (i.e., disease), and wild animal attacks (Revelation 6:8).

Some experts argue that all of these things will be natural consequences of the Second and Third Seal judgments. If there will be an outbreak of wars and people are unable to afford enough food to eat, many people might begin to use violence to steal resources from each other.

Jesus warned that in the last days there will be an increase of lawlessness, and people's love for others will disappear (Matthew 24:12). When war, economic disaster, and famine make food and resources scarce, many people will turn to violence to provide for themselves and their families.

Pestilence and animal attacks could likewise be seen as effects of people not having enough food.

If people are malnourished, their bodies cannot fight off diseases as effectively. If people die at a faster rate than their bodies can be buried or cremated, and morgues run out of storage space, the rotting bodies will also lead to an increase of disease.

Also, if there is not enough food, many people might forage for food in the wild. This could lead to people being attacked by animals, especially if the animals are also hungry because people are eating the food that normally the animals would eat.

Some Bible prophecy experts believe that this Fourth Seal judgment means that up to a quarter of the world's population will die from the above causes. Others claim that it will only be a quarter of the world that will be affected by these problems, but not a quarter of all people will die.

Some prophecy experts believe that the total deaths in the Fourth Seal judgment could include all of those people who will die in the Second and Third Seal judgments. Other experts believe the Fourth Seal is a separate judgment that will kill a quarter of everyone who has survived the Second and Third Seal judgments.

Regardless of which view will be correct, the loss of life during the Fourth Seal judgment will be very significant. This loss of this many people may cause even more chaos for the world than the Rapture will.

The Fifth Seal Judgment and Babylon the Great

The Fifth Seal judgment appears to be a dramatic increase in Christians being killed for their faith (Revelation 6:9).

But this is not the end of persecution or martyrdom during the Tribulation, which will continue and increase once the Antichrist gains even greater power. So the martyrs are told to rest and wait for a while, until all the rest of those people who will be killed for their faith during the Tribulation will join them in Heaven (Revelation 6:10–11).

Perhaps this persecution of Christians will increase because of something that is referred to as "Babylon."

It must be noted that this "Babylon" is not referring to the actual city named Babylon that is currently in the country of Iraq, and "Babylon" is also not the same as the historical Babylonian Empire.

This "Babylon" in the Book of Revelation is symbolically represented as a woman who rides (i.e., who is supported by and partly controls) a "beast," for at least some period of time (Revelation 17:1–4).

This "beast" will be discussed in more detail in the next chapter, but for now, it is enough to say that the beast represents the Antichrist's world government/empire.

"Babylon" is described metaphorically as being a "prostitute" or "harlot" that many world leaders and other people around the world have had immoral relations with (Revelation 17:1–2). In the Bible, prostitution is often used as a metaphor for spiritual adultery, which is when people worship other gods or things that are not God.

For example, God instructed the prophet Hosea to marry and have a family with a woman who was actively working as a prostitute (Hosea 1:2–3). The purpose of this strange instruction was so that God could teach the people of Hosea's time about God's love for them and his faithfulness to them, despite how they were following other gods. It was also a promise that God would one day bring his people back to being faithful to God (Hosea 2:14–23).

The same analogy is also used in Ezekiel chapter 16, where Israel is described as a bride who was engaged to God and was given many fine gifts from God, but who went astray and became a prostitute. This described how the country was looking for protection and security by making alliances with other surrounding nations, rather than trusting in God (Ezekiel 16:26–34). The people were also led into idolatry and many immoral practices that were represented as spiritual adultery (Ezekiel 16:15–25).

Therefore, if "Babylon" is symbolically represented as a prostitute, it seems that whatever "Babylon" will actually be, it will have something to do with convincing the leaders of the world and the rest of the people to worship something that is not God, and to commit other immoral acts.

"Babylon" is also symbolically described as being drunk on the blood of the martyrs and saints (Revelation 17:5–6). This is most likely because of how it will persecute and murder many people who will believe in Jesus after the Rapture.

Later on, the Antichrist will make war on the saints who put their faith in Jesus after the Rapture (Revelation 13:7). But it seems that "Babylon" will be doing part of the work for him for some period of time before the Antichrist and ten other world leaders who run the one-world "beast" government will turn against "Babylon" and destroy it (Revelation 17:12–16).

More will be said about the possible identity of "Babylon" in the coming chapters.

The Sixth Seal Judgment

The Sixth Seal judgment sounds like it will be some sort of astronomical disaster that affects the entire planet.

There will be an earthquake, the Sun will become dark, the Moon will turn blood-red, and "stars" will fall to Earth, in a way that is reminiscent of how figs fall off fig trees during a strong wind. The sky will appear to roll up like a scroll, and every mountain and island will be moved from their places (Revelation 6:12–14).

It seems the world will have had some advance notice about what is coming, because everyone will hide in caves and among the mountains, even the rich and powerful people of the world (Revelation 6:15).

The people will finally recognize that this disaster is a demonstration of God's wrath, because they are so afraid that they would rather have the mountains fall on them than face this divine judgment (Revelation 6:16–17).

The somewhat-unusual descriptions make this judgment hard to understand. However, if one thinks back to popular movies in the 1990s about asteroids that impact Earth, perhaps it makes more sense. If a very large asteroid or a rogue planet were to have a near-miss with Earth, all of the above effects might theoretically be achieved.

Such a large asteroid or rogue planet could perhaps be dragging along many smaller asteroids in its gravity. These could be pulled in by Earth's stronger gravity, and would become meteorites that cause many large explosions when they impact the Earth, even if the larger asteroid or planet itself misses Earth.

Dirt, dust, and ash in the atmosphere from the meteorite impacts could block out the Sun's rays and make the Moon appear to turn red, as can happen during volcanic explosions, or when forest fires put ash into the sky. If volcanos will be triggered due to the stress on Earth's tectonic plates during this judgment, this ash might also contribute to the darkness.

The sky might also look like it rolls up in a scroll, thanks to how the clouds could form rolls due to the shockwaves of the impacting meteorites, as happens in nuclear explosions.

If the mass of the asteroid or rogue planet that nearly misses Earth is large enough, it could theoretically shift Earth's axis slightly, causing all the mountains and islands (i.e., all geological landmarks) to now have different geographic coordinates, so that they are all "moved from their places."

During such a catastrophe, large caves or bunkers deep underground may be the safest places to be. Some people speculate that governments around the world have already built such facilities in case of a disaster like this.

However, all of the above is speculation, even if it does seem like it could be a scientific explanation for what John saw in his vision. Perhaps this judgment will actually be caused by something else. Again, only the people who will be alive on Earth during that time will know for sure.

Regardless, as a result of this terrifying Sixth Seal judgment, the people of the world finally realize that they are facing God's divine judgment (Revelation 6:16–17).

After the Sixth Seal, there is a brief pause in the judgments while 144,000 Jews are sealed on their foreheads with God's divine protection, including 12,000 Jews from each of the twelve tribes of Israel (Revelation 7:1–8). These Jews are described later in the Book of Revelation as all being male virgins who will faithfully follow Jesus (Revelation 14:1–5).

Many prophecy experts believe these Jews will become missionaries to the rest of the world during the Tribulation. As a result, millions of people from every tribe and nation and language will be eternally saved by believing that Jesus died for their sins (Revelation 7:9–17).

Most likely, the "seals" on the 144,000's foreheads will not be literal, visible seals. Instead, these seals may only be visible in the spiritual dimension. For example, in the Old Testament, before the destruction of Jerusalem by the Babylonian Empire, God told an angel to put spiritual "marks" on the foreheads of anyone who sighed or groaned due to the sins that occurred in their city (Ezekiel 9:4). These people's lives would be miraculously spared, while the rest of the people would be killed (Ezekiel 9:5–7).

It might be these 144,000 Jews who are spoken about by Jesus at the Sheep and Goats Judgment as being Christ's "brothers." They will need the food, water, shelter, and clothing that the faithful saints will provide for them during the Tribulation (Matthew 25:34–40). More will be said about this in chapter 8.

The Seventh Seal Judgment

The Seventh Seal judgment opens with silence for half an hour in Heaven, while the next seven Trumpet judgments are prepared (Revelation 8:1–6). This silence signifies that something serious is happening, because usually in Heaven, worship of God goes on continually (Revelation 4:1–8).

This Seventh Seal judgment also involves an angel throwing heavenly "fire" on the Earth, leading to lightning, thunder, and an earthquake (Revelation 8:3–5).

Some prophecy experts say that the twenty-one judgments of the Book of Revelation do not happen in a linear sequence. Instead, they might say that the three sets of seven judgments represented by the Seals, Trumpets, and Bowls are just different ways of describing the same seven divine judgments.

This argument relies on a few small similarities between some of the judgments. Those prophecy experts who take this view also usually believe that the Sixth Seal judgment is so terrible that it must happen at the end of the Tribulation.

However, it seems clear in the text that the Seventh Seal judgment unlocks the next series of seven Trumpet judgments (Revelation 8:1–2). Therefore, even though the first seven Seal judgments were terrible, it does not mean that they have to occur only at the end of the Tribulation.

Most people will likely safely come out of their hiding places after the Sixth Seal judgment. They will return to their homes and lives, having survived what they thought would be a world-ending disaster.

Although some things will be destroyed from the falling "stars" that could be meteorite impacts (Revelation 6:13), there will be enough of the world's infrastructure left that repairs will be able to be made, and global society will continue on much like it did before.

This must be true, because certain technologies will have to be functional to fulfill certain prophecies about what will happen later on during the Tribulation. Thus, the Sixth Seal will not destroy society, and it will not send the world back to the level of technology found in the Middle Ages, or even earlier.

For example, a global network of digital financial transactions seems to be a necessary part of the Mark of the Beast, which is how the Antichrist will control the whole world (Revelation 13:16–18). As will be described more in Chapter 7, this system will likely be implemented halfway through the seven-year Tribulation period.

Worldwide live video broadcasting also seems to be necessary in order for the entire world to see the deaths and resurrections of the Two Witnesses in Revelation chapter 11.

THE TWO WITNESSES

The Two Witnesses are two individuals who will act very much like the prophets in the Old Testament, who spoke God's word to the people and called them to repent from their sins.

During the time they are prophesying, the Two Witnesses will be able to cause droughts, turn water into blood, and cause plagues on the Earth (Revelation 11:1–6). They will have miraculous powers to destroy anyone who threatens them, except for the Antichrist, who will finally kill them (Revelation 11:7).

Their dead bodies will remain in the streets of Jerusalem, and the entire world will be able to see their bodies lying there for three and a half days (Revelation 11:8–9). This suggests that live video of the dead prophets will be available around the world. This event is an interesting fact that shows this prophecy could only be fulfilled after worldwide live video communication technology had been invented.

During the three days after the Two Witnesses are killed, the world will celebrate that these two individuals who have caused everyone so much suffering are now dead. People will be so happy that they will even give presents to each other (Revelation 11:10).

But after three-and-a-half days, the Two Witnesses will come back to life, and will be taken up into Heaven in their own personal Rapture-like event (Revelation 11:11–12). At the same time, an earthquake will flatten a tenth of the city of Jerusalem, and seven thousand people will die (Revelation 11:13).

These Two Witnesses will likely appear very soon after the start of the Tribulation, because it seems that they will prophesy for 1,260 days before being killed by the Antichrist after the Sixth Trumpet Judgment (Revelation 11:3, 11:12–14). Their deaths may occur shortly after the Antichrist will appear to die from being wounded by a sword, seem to come back to life

(Revelation 11:7, 13:2–5, 13:12–14, 17:8–11), and then declare himself to be God in the rebuilt Temple in Jerusalem, halfway through the Tribulation (2 Thessalonians 2:3–4, Daniel 9:27). More will be said about this later.

In addition to the above Bible verses, it seems that all of this will happen halfway through the Tribulation because it is unlikely that the people of the world will be able to buy gifts for each other at the end of the Tribulation, when the world has been almost completely destroyed by the Bowl judgments.

At the half-way point of the Tribulation there will still be enough of a functioning economy that this behavior seems more plausible. It is also doubtful whether the world will have a functioning power grid after the Fourth and Fifth Bowl judgments, to enable worldwide video broadcasting of the Two Witnesses' dead bodies (Revelation 11:9).

Some prophecy experts may disagree with this timeline regarding the ministry of the Two Witnesses. The exact timing of the deaths of the Two Witnesses is not extremely important, but once they appear, it will be obvious who they are, and how long they will prophesy for.

The Trumpet Judgments

The seven Trumpet judgments are depicted symbolically as seven angels that blow seven different trumpets, one after another.

These judgments are described in a more straightforward manner than the Seal Judgments are. Yet it is also more difficult to speculate about what it could be that will cause the Trumpet judgments, from a human or scientific perspective. However, the effects of these judgments will be very destructive to the world.

The First Trumpet judgment will involve hail, fire, and "blood" being thrown down onto the world. As a result, a third of the Earth's surface and a third of the world's trees will be burned up. All green grass will also be burned up (Revelation 8:7).

The Second Trumpet judgment involves some sort of huge burning "mountain" being thrown into the sea. A third of the oceans will become like blood, a third of all living creatures in the sea will die, and it seems that a third of the world's ships will be destroyed (Revelation 8:8–9).

Based on this description, many prophecy experts have claimed that the Second Trumpet judgment could be another asteroid impact, or maybe a nuclear explosion somewhere in the ocean. However, nuclear explosions are not this powerful, so an asteroid impact seems more likely.

This asteroid will likely be larger than the meteorites that might fall in the Sixth Seal judgment, but because this asteroid impacts the ocean, it could cause less damage overall than if it were to impact land.

As a result, though, a third of the world's ships will be destroyed, perhaps through the huge tsunami that such an asteroid impact in the ocean would produce. The Pacific Ocean contains many cargo ships due to trade between Asia and North America, so perhaps this will be the ocean that is impacted by the asteroid.

However, it is not clear how such an asteroid impact could turn a third of the ocean into blood (Revelation 8:8). This part of the Second Trumpet judgment reminds Bible commentators of the judgments that God sent upon Egypt through the prophet Moses.

The first of these judgments involved all the water in the land of Egypt being turned into blood—even the water that was inside sealed containers. All of the fish in the Nile died as a result, and the people had to dig new wells to get drinking water (Exodus 7:17–23).

Some scientists who study the judgments that are described in the Book of Exodus try to find scientific explanations for them. For example, the "blood" that filled the Nile is sometimes thought to have been a reddish algae that made the water toxic to the fish and the people.

However, others debunk this explanation, and prefer to say it was truly a divine miracle that literally turned the water into blood. The fact that the water even inside sealed containers changed to blood seems to show it was something supernatural that caused this effect.

During the Tribulation, it will be only those unfortunate people who are alive during this judgment who will fully understand whether the water will become real blood, or only something else toxic that resembles blood.

The Third Trumpet judgment will involve another fiery "star" falling to Earth. This star will be named "Wormwood," which is also the name of a bitter-tasting plant that is found in the Middle East. This plant is sometimes consumed for flavoring in alcohols or is used as medicine, but it can also be toxic, depending on the dosage. The Bible says this "star" will impact a third of Earth's fresh water, and turn the water so bitter that many people who drink it will die (Revelation 8:10–11).

It is unclear whether there is some location that a falling asteroid, meteorite, satellite, or nuclear weapon could impact that would taint a third of the world's fresh drinking water. Maybe there is such a location. Or, perhaps the effect will be more distributed, and a third of the drinking water over the entire world will be affected.

Some scientists have noted that if an asteroid or meteorite containing enough of a mineral like sulfur were to enter Earth's atmosphere, it could potentially break up. This would disperse the sulfur into the air, where it could mix into clouds and return to Earth as acid rain. In this way, an asteroid or meteor could theoretically contaminate freshwater lakes and rivers over large areas of the planet.

This Third Trumpet judgment is reminiscent of the incident when the Israelites crossed the Red Sea and came to the springs called Marah. The water there was so bitter that they were unable to drink it, until God performed a miracle through Moses that changed the water to become drinkable (Exodus 15:22–26). But no one was recorded as dying from drinking that water, so it seems that the Third Trumpet judgment will be quite awful indeed.

The Fourth Trumpet judgment will somehow block out a third of the light of the Sun, a third of the light of the Moon, and a third of the light of the stars (Revelation 8:12). This could be due to some sort of dust or debris that enters the upper atmosphere, and so dims all the light coming through it to be only two-thirds as intense as before.

But John's description of the Fourth Trumpet judgment also includes the details that the sun will not shine during a third of the day, and the moon and stars will not shine during a third of the night. It is not clear what could cause this sort of effect, but again, the people who will be alive during this time will know exactly what it is.

The final three Trumpet judgments are also called the "three woes," due to the intense suffering they will cause the people of Earth (Revelation 8:13, 9:12). These next three judgments also seem to be supernatural, rather than mostly-natural disasters like the judgments that have happened so far.

The Fifth Trumpet judgment involves a "star" that seems to be personified as a "he," who has a key to open the "bottomless pit" (called the "abyss" in the original Greek). As a result, smoke pours out of the abyss that darkens the air, and some sort of demonic locusts come out that will have the ability to sting people like scorpions do (Revelation 9:1–3).

For five months, these locusts will torment everyone who does not have the seal of God's divine protection on their foreheads. The people who will be tormented by the locusts will want to die, but they will somehow be unable to do so (Revelation 9:4–6).

The description of these locusts is quite unusual, and Bible prophecy experts do not currently understand what all these details mean (Revelation 9:7–10). These locusts are described as having a leader named Abaddon or Apollyon, who is identified as the "king" of the "bottomless pit" (Revelation 9:11). So it seems these "locusts" truly are some sort of demonic entities, and not just regular insects or even genetically modified insects.

Some Bible commentators identify the "bottomless pit" as *Tartarus*. This is the term used by Peter to describe the location where some particularly evil fallen angels have been confined by God ever since the time of the worldwide Flood (2 Peter 2:4–5). The same concept is mentioned also by Jude (Jude 1:6).

Similarly, the Greeks believed that Tartarus was a location where some of the especially powerful beings called Titans were confined by Zeus and other Greek gods after they defeated the Titans in a war. Perhaps this Greek myth was a corruption of the truth that had been passed down to Peter and Jude through the Old Testament or other Israelite traditions.

Regardless, if the Tartarus mentioned in 2 Peter 2:4–5 is the same as this "bottomless pit" in Revelation 9:1–2, then it provides additional support for the idea that these "locusts" in Revelation 9:3–11 are demonic beings.

The Sixth Trumpet also seems to be something supernatural. During this judgment, four angels that have been bound somewhere near the Euphrates River will be released.

The Bible says these angels were prepared for this exact time, and they will kill a third of everyone who has managed to stay alive this far into the Tribulation. These deaths will be caused by fire, smoke, and sulfur

(Revelation 9:13–15, 9:18). Exactly what produces the fire, smoke, and sulfur, though, is less clear.

Like in the description of the demonic locusts from the Fifth Trumpet judgment, the description of the Sixth Trumpet judgment seems to portray an army of soldiers mounted on horses. But these are not normal horses, since they have heads like lions. Their mouths produce fire, smoke, and sulfur, while their tails are like serpents that wound people (Revelation 9:16–19).

The Bible says there will be two hundred million of these soldiers on strange horses that will be led by the four angels that will come from the Euphrates River (Revelation 9:15–16).

There has been much speculation over what this judgment portrays. Some prophecy experts have interpreted it as a vast human army, and have argued that certain heavily-populated countries on the Eastern side of the Euphrates River may be able to form an army this large. Other experts argue that this judgment describes nuclear war, because of the fire, smoke, and sulfur that kills a third of the world's people. But it is not clear, and probably only the people who are alive on Earth during this judgment will know exactly what the Bible is describing.

Despite the severity of these two "woe" judgments (the Fifth and Sixth Trumpet judgments), the Bible says that those who survive will still not turn away from their sins. These sins will include worshiping demons, idolatry, murder, sorcery, sexual immorality, and stealing (Revelation 9:20–21).

There is a clue as to the timing of the Sixth Trumpet judgment, because the second "woe" judgment is mentioned in connection to the deaths and resurrections of the Two Witnesses in Jerusalem (Revelation 11:14). They will have been prophesying there for 1,260 days, until they seem to be killed by the Antichrist (Revelation 11:3–8).

This is another hint that the twenty-one judgments in Revelation are sequential, and so they are not just the same events being described in different ways.

Due to how the timing lines up so well, it appears that the 1,260 days during which the Two Witnesses will prophesy will come to an end at the midpoint of the Tribulation.

The Midpoint of the Tribulation

At the midpoint of the Tribulation, it is likely that several important things will happen within a short period of time.

The Antichrist will probably appear to be killed by a sword. However, he will seem to come back to life (Revelation 13:3–4, 13:12–14), and then declare himself to be God in the rebuilt Temple in Jerusalem (2 Thessalonians 2:3–4).

This action by the Antichrist will desecrate the Temple and stop the sacrifices that had been going on there until that point, in an event called the *Abomination of Desolation* (Matthew 24:15, Daniel 9:27, 8:9–14).

Jesus warned that everyone who is living in Judea at that time should immediately flee to the mountains in order to protect their lives, without stopping to pack supplies or even grab their coats (Matthew 24:15–18, Mark 13:14–16, Luke 17:22–35).

Shortly after this, Antichrist will successfully kill the Two Witnesses who will also be in Jerusalem. This action will make the world celebrate and give gifts to each other (Revelation 11:10). This action will also likely appear to verify the Antichrist's indestructibility to the people of the world, because until that point, no one else had been able to harm the Two Witnesses due to their miraculous abilities to defend themselves (Revelation 13:3–4, 11:5–10).

This apparent "miracle," in addition to the Antichrist's pseudo-resurrection, would further solidify the "divine" status of the Antichrist in the minds of the people of the world, and they will worship him (Revelation 13:4, 13:8).

Following this, the Antichrist will rise to even greater levels of world influence for the next forty-two months (Revelation 13:5). He will attempt to destroy everyone who opposes him and does not worship him, such as the saints who will believe in Jesus after the Rapture (Revelation 13:7, 13:15, 20:4).

It is also then that the Antichrist and ten other world rulers will probably destroy the false world religion called "Babylon" that had previously been supported by and had partial control of the Antichrist's world government (Revelation 17:16–17). "Babylon" will be replaced by the Antichrist's own religion and economic system that will require everyone to take the Mark of the Beast or be cut off from all ability to buy and sell (Revelation 13:16–18).

The Image of the Beast will also be created. It seems it will be an idol of the Antichrist that will appear to be able to speak, and also able to somehow kill anyone who refuses to worship it (Revelation 13:13–15).

Therefore, at the midpoint of the Tribulation, the Antichrist will become the most powerful person on the planet, and he will have the full support of Satan and the False Prophet. The Antichrist will insist on being worshipped, and he will persecute and kill many people who will refuse to do so.

More will be said on these topics in the next chapter. For now, the discussion will return to the last few divine judgments.

The Seventh Trumpet Judgment

The Seventh Trumpet judgment announces the soon-to-be-coming kingdom of Jesus Christ. It is accompanied by lightning, thunder, an earthquake, and heavy hail falling upon the Earth (Revelation 11:15–19).

It may include another Rapture-like event to rescue the 144,000 converted Jewish evangelists who had been sealed with divine protection after the Sixth Seal judgment (Revelation 7:1–4). This is because the 144,000 are now described as having been redeemed from the Earth, and as standing on Mount Zion with "the Lamb," which is a reference to Jesus (Revelation 14:1–3, Revelation 5:1–13). Mount Zion appears to still be in Heaven at that point, because Jesus will not return to Earth until his Second Coming, which will be forty-two months away (Revelation 13:5).

More evidence to support this interpretation comes from the Book of Hebrews. There, Mount Zion is called the heavenly dwelling place of God, the heavenly Jerusalem, and many angels and saints live there, along with Jesus (Hebrews 12:22–24). During the Tribulation, this heavenly Mount Zion will also be where all the Christians who were resurrected and raptured will be living, in the dwelling places that Jesus had prepared for them (John 14:1–3).

It is true that the earthly city of Jerusalem will be raised up to become a mountain called Zion at Jesus' Second Coming, when his feet will touch the Mount of Olives (Zechariah 8:3, 14:1–11).

Yet it is only after the thousand-year Millennial Kingdom of Jesus and the Final Judgment (Revelation 20) that the New Jerusalem will come down to the New Earth, and then God will live with his people on the New Earth forever (Revelation 21:1–3, see also Micah 4:1–7 and Joel 3:17).

The Bowl Judgments

Before the Bowl judgments begin, several things will happen.

First, it appears there will be war in Heaven, and Satan and his demons will be thrown down to Earth (Revelation 12:7–10). Satan will be very angry, because he will know that he only has forty-two months before Jesus' Second Coming. When that happens, he will be locked up in the supernatural jail called the "bottomless pit" for a thousand years during Jesus' Millennial Kingdom (Revelation 20:1–3).

Satan will help the Antichrist in his war against the saints (Revelation 12:13–17, 13:7). This war will likely begin around the time when the Antichrist appears to come back to life and will declare himself to be God in the Temple (2 Thessalonians 2:3–4, Revelation 13:3–4).

Next, three angels will fly overhead with different messages for the people of the world during the last half of the Tribulation.

The first angel will proclaim the gospel to everyone who is still alive, in every nation, to every people group, and in every language (Revelation 14:6–7). This will fulfill Jesus' prophecy that before the end comes, the gospel will be preached to all people in the world (Matthew 24:14).

The second angel will proclaim that "Babylon" has fallen (Revelation 14:8). This confirms that "Babylon" will be destroyed by the Antichrist and the ten kings at the halfway point of the Tribulation (Revelation 17:16–17).

The third angel will warn everyone about what the horrible consequences will be if they take the Mark of the Beast.

It seems these consequences may involve eternal torment, or at least torment that does not cease for as long as God has determined it should last (Revelation 14:9–11). So it is *very* important for people to know this before they choose to worship the Antichrist or his Image and take his Mark.

After the Seal and Trumpet judgments, the world has reached the point that it is deemed to be fully ripe for God's most severe judgment (Revelation

14:14–16). The final seven divine judgments that will come upon the Earth are symbolically depicted as angels pouring out bowls of God's wrath onto the planet.

Together, the Bowl judgments will cause so many deaths that they can be symbolically represented as God's angels using sickles to harvest people as if they were grapes that would then be crushed in a winepress. Therefore, instead of grape juice, the combined result of these judgments will be an extreme amount of blood (i.e., death) (Revelation 14:17–20).

The First Bowl judgment will cause painful sores to break out on the skin of those who took the Mark of the Beast and worshiped the Image of the Beast (Revelation 16:2).

The Second Bowl judgment will complete what had begun in the Second Trumpet judgment. Then, only a third of the world's oceans turned to blood (Revelation 8:8–9). Now, *all* of the oceans will turn into something resembling the blood of a corpse, and all the sea creatures will die (Revelation 16:3).

The Third Bowl judgment will complete what began in the Third Trumpet judgment. Then, a star fell that made a third of the world's fresh water become so bitter that people died when they drank it (Revelation 8:10–11). Now, *all* the streams and rivers will become blood, just like the oceans will be.

Once this occurs, it seems there will be no drinkable water left on the planet. Yet people can only survive for approximately three days without water. So perhaps the people on Earth will find some way to filter the "blood" so that it will be drinkable. Or maybe they will rely on pre-packaged beverages to survive. Or maybe the "blood" actually will be drinkable, even if it is disgusting. Only the people who are unfortunate enough to be alive at the time will know for sure.

The Fourth Bowl judgment will cause the Sun to scorch people with intense heat and fire. The people will curse God, but still refuse to repent from their sins (Revelation 16:8–9).

The Fifth Bowl judgment will plunge the Antichrist's kingdom into darkness that causes another form of anguish. The people will still be suffering from the sores caused by the First Bowl judgment, but still, they will curse God and not repent from their sins (Revelation 16:10–11).

The Fifth Bowl judgment reminds Bible commentators of the plague of darkness that was the ninth plague of Egypt before the Pharaoh let Moses and the Israelites leave. This darkness was so intense that it could actually be *felt*, and no one could get up or do anything for three days (Exodus 10:21–23).

The Sixth Bowl judgment will dry up the Euphrates River completely, in order to allow kings from the east to cross it (Revelation 16:12).

These kings seem to come at the Antichrist's request, because they are summoned to come by three demonic spirits that resemble frogs. These spirits are sent out to gather the leaders from around the entire world and the world's armies to prepare for the Battle of *Armageddon*, (a.k.a., *Harmageddon* or *Har Megiddo*) (Revelation 16:13–16).

This battle will take place in northern Israel, at the place called *Har Megiddo*, which is about fifty-five miles or eighty-nine kilometers north of Jerusalem.

Although *Har* is translated as "Mount," Megiddo is (at least currently) only a mound of rubble that archaeologists called a *Tel*, which contains the ruins of several ancient cities that have been built, destroyed, and rebuilt at the same location.

Tel Megiddo is located in a very large and flat region of Israel, where at least one major Old-Testament battle was fought (2 Chronicles 35:22). It is easy to imagine vast armies lining up their divisions into formation in this region, in order to make a final attempt to prevent Jesus' Second Coming, which will occur at Jerusalem.

As a side note, it seems unusual that demonic spirits would be necessary to summon the world's leaders and their militaries to come to the Battle of Armageddon (Revelation 16:13–16).

Perhaps this is a clue that by this point in the Tribulation, much of the world's telecommunications network might have been destroyed or incapacitated.

Otherwise, the Antichrist could just call, email, text, or video chat with these leaders.

It is possible that the destruction of the world's communication systems will have occurred during the earlier Fourth Bowl judgment, when the Sun will scorch people with fire and heat (Revelation 16:8–9).

It is the Earth's magnetic field that protects all life on Earth from harmful solar radiation. If a strong solar flare were to disrupt Earth's magnetic field enough, then solar radiation could negatively affect people on the surface, possibly resulting in severe radiation burns, which a sunburn is a mild version of.

A strong solar flare could also cause electromagnetic interference that could destroy unshielded electronic equipment. This destructive effect of solar flares was demonstrated in 1859 during what is now called the Carrington Event. During this event, a solar storm caused solar flares that reached Earth and destroyed telegraph wires and equipment.

Many experts worry that if Earth were ever to be directly hit by a strong solar flare, it could destroy large parts of the world's power grid, and induce electric currents that would damage many electronic devices. Depending on how widespread the damage would be, it could possibly set the world back to a pre-modern level of communication. In that state, there would be no way for the Antichrist to send messages quickly all around the world, except by supernatural demonic couriers.

If the Fourth Bowl judgment is an extremely powerful solar flare, it could also explain the Fifth Bowl judgment that plunges the Antichrist's empire into darkness (Revelation 16:10–11). His empire will likely rely on a worldwide communications network and digital technology in order to control all buying and selling through the Mark of the Beast (Revelation 13:16–17).

Therefore, if the planet's entire power grid were to collapse due to a giant solar storm or solar flare, it would bring "darkness" to the planet because no one would have electricity. This would be a severe problem for such an advanced society, and could certainly cause much anguish (Revelation 16:10–11).

The Seventh Bowl judgment is the final divine judgment of the Tribulation period. It will involve lightning, thunder, and the strongest earthquake that has ever happened. Jerusalem will be split into three parts, and many other cities around the world will be completely destroyed. Hailstones that weigh a hundred pounds each will also fall on people (Revelation 16:17–21).

It seems that one of these cities that will be affected is Rome, where "Babylon" was headquartered, as a final end to God's judgment on "Babylon" (Revelation 16:19, 17:9, 17:18). This destruction will finish off how the Antichrist and the ten world leaders under the Antichrist's command destroyed "Babylon" with fire earlier in the Tribulation period (Revelation 17:16–17).

After the Seventh Bowl judgment is when Jesus' Second Coming will occur. All the armies of the world will be destroyed during the Battle of Armageddon (Revelation 19:11–21). This event will be discussed in more detail in Chapter 8.

This concludes the discussion of the twenty-one divine judgments that the world will experience during the Tribulation period. However, there are still some details that have not yet been fully explained.

For example:

- Why is the Antichrist and/or his government represented symbolically as a "beast"?
- How will people know who the Antichrist is, in order to avoid being deceived by him?
- What is it that the Book of Revelation is representing through the symbol of the prostitute named "Babylon," which seems to be related to the city of Rome?
- Who will be the False Prophet who will support and do miracles for the Antichrist?

Possible answers to these questions will be explored in more detail in the next two chapters.

Chapter 5

The Antichrist, His Empire, Babylon, and the Abomination of Desolation

During the seven-year Tribulation, two individuals will rise up and gain significant power over the whole world. Bible prophecy experts call these two individuals the Antichrist and the False Prophet.

Both of these men will be working for Satan, and they will be empowered by Satan to perform many amazingly deceptive feats (2 Thessalonians 2:9–10, Matthew 24:24, Revelation 13:2, 13:11–14).

Together, Satan, the Antichrist, and the False Prophet will form an "unholy trinity." This will be Satan's attempt to impersonate the true Trinity of God the Father, God the Son (Jesus Christ), and the Holy Spirit.

Therefore, the Antichrist and the False Prophet will be very deceptive. They will not openly announce who they are by using these titles, and so they must be identified based on what the Bible says about them.

This chapter and the next will examine what the Bible says about these two men, in the hope of making it easy for those who will live during the Tribulation to identify these dangerous individuals and reject their lies.

THE BIBLE WARNS ABOUT MANY ANTICHRISTS AND FALSE PROPHETS

Jesus warned that many deceptive people would attempt to impersonate the Messiah in the last days. Their deceptions will be so convincing that many people will think they truly are who they claim to be, and so they will gain many followers (Matthew 24:24, Mark 13:22).

The Apostle John also warned that many antichrists would come in the last days, beginning even in John's time (1 John 2:18). These antichrists will be identifiable because they will deny that Jesus was truly God's Son. They will also deny that Jesus was the promised *Anointed One* that God sent into the world (1 John 2:22–23, 4:3, 2 John 1:7).

In ancient Greek, the word used for "the Anointed One" is *christos*, translated into English as "Christ." In

Hebrew, the word is *ha maschiah*, translated into English as "the Messiah."

Anointing someone by putting specially-made oil on their head was how both priests and kings were appointed in the Old Testament (e.g., 1 Samuel 10:1, 16:13, 2 Samuel 5:17, Exodus 30:22–38, Leviticus 16:32).

Jesus is God's Son, and thus, he is the ultimate Anointed One (Luke 4:18, Psalm 2:1–12). Jesus will be both the final eternal King, and the world's High Priest, just like how a mysterious Old Testament figure named Melchizedek was both a king and a priest in the ancient city that became Jerusalem (Hebrews 5:5–10, 7:1–28).

So anyone who claims to be the Christ or the Messiah is claiming to be the "Anointed One," the one who was chosen by God to be his special servant, messenger, and ultimately, the rightful ruler of the world.

It will be easy to determine if anyone who claims to be the Christ or the Messiah is lying. This is because when Jesus Christ will return to Earth at his Second Coming, it will be as obvious and clear as lightning that flashes from one side of the sky to the other (Luke 17:23–24, Matthew 24:24–27). He will appear in the clouds and will be riding on a white horse, and everyone will see him (Revelation 1:7).

Jesus will be wearing many crowns on his head and a robe dipped in or covered with blood (Revelation

19:11–13). Armies from Heaven will accompany him, and Jesus will defeat the earthly armies that have gathered to oppose him at the Battle of Armageddon (Revelation 19:14). In this way, Jesus's Second Coming will be similar to how he left Earth, when he ascended from Earth to the clouds, and then into Heaven (Acts 1:11), but this time, he will travel in the opposite direction.

So Jesus will *not* be born again or be reincarnated into some new body. Do not believe anyone who claims to be Jesus if he does not appear in the clouds, on a white horse, with the armies of Heaven following him!

Unfortunately, many people do not understand that this is how Jesus' Second Coming will occur, because they do not know what the Bible teaches on this topic. Such people will be easily deceived by the Antichrist and False Prophet's miracles, and they will believe that the Antichrist actually is the world's Messiah. Jesus warned that people who reject him and who love unrighteousness will accept the Antichrist as the Christ/Messiah (John 5:43, 2 Thessalonians 2:9–12).

It is true that the word *antichrist* is not used anywhere in the Book of Revelation. But as seen earlier, the term *antichrist* is used elsewhere in the Bible to describe anyone who denies that Jesus is the Christ/Messiah and instead portrays themselves as the Christ/Messiah.

The man who will appear on the world scene during the Tribulation and who will falsely claim to be God will be the ultimate example of all those previous antichrists and false messiahs who have come before in history. Therefore, this man is commonly referred to by Bible prophecy experts as *the Antichrist*.

However, there are some very specific traits of the Antichrist that will make him even easier to identify by anyone who is alive during the Tribulation, if they know what to look for.

The Antichrist

The first clue that will identify the Antichrist is that the Bible says he will rise to power after the Church has been raptured (2 Thessalonians 2:3–7). Therefore, it is unlikely that the Antichrist will be anyone who is well-known to the public before the Rapture, such as a celebrity or an influential world leader.

As was discussed in the previous chapter, the Antichrist will most likely be revealed during the First Seal judgment. He will appear to have already conquered or been victorious in some way, and he will conquer even more in the future (Revelation 6:1–2).

The Antichrist will seem to be a savior-like figure that the entire world will look to during the chaotic aftermath of the Rapture. The most important clue to the Antichrist's identity is that he will sign or confirm or strengthen some sort of covenant or peace treaty with Israel and "many" (Daniel 9:27).

Eventually, the Antichrist will gain power over the entire world. He will receive this power from Satan (Revelation 13:2–8).

During Jesus' temptation in the wilderness, Satan approached Jesus and attempted to get Jesus to sin by worshipping Satan. If Jesus would only worship Satan, Satan said he would give Jesus power over all the kingdoms of the world, because temporarily, the world is under Satan's power (Luke 4:5–7, John 14:30–31, 12:31). So it seems that the Antichrist will accept the offer from Satan that Jesus rejected.

The Bible tells us about the rise of the Antichrist in several different places. Yet the Antichrist will be preceded by the formation of an empire that will dominate the whole world during the Tribulation.

So, before examining what the Bible says about the specific actions of the Antichrist, it is valuable to examine what the Bible says the final world empire will be like during the last days.

THE FINAL "REVIVED" ROMAN EMPIRE

During the Tribulation, the Bible predicts that there will be a large empire that will come to be controlled by the Antichrist.

It will have power over the whole world. It will also be the last empire the world will see before Jesus' Millennial Kingdom.

Prophecy experts often believe that this last world empire will have some similarities to the ancient Roman Empire, for a number of reasons. Thus, Bible prophecy experts sometimes call this final world empire the *Revived Roman Empire.*

For example, the Antichrist is described as being a prince who will come from the same people as those who destroyed the second Temple in Jerusalem (Daniel 9:26). This destruction occurred in 70 AD, and the army was led by the Roman general Titus, who later went on to become a Roman emperor.

Therefore, many prophecy experts believe that the man who will become the Antichrist will come from one of the regions that was part of the ancient Roman Empire. Or maybe he will be able to trace his lineage back to the ancient Roman people. He could possibly even come from the city of Rome itself, or set up his headquarters there.

Additionally, the Antichrist will likely gain power over the same regions that historically made up parts of the ancient Roman Empire, such as Europe, North Africa, and the regions surrounding the Mediterranean Sea. Therefore, it might seem to the world as if the Roman Empire has been revived after it disappeared from the world stage for many centuries.

This Revived Roman Empire is seen in the prophet Daniel's description of a statue that appeared in one of the Babylonian King Nebuchadnezzar's dreams.

In Nebuchadnezzar's dream, he saw a large statue that looked like a man. Different portions of the statue were made of different types of materials, representing several empires that would successively have power over the land of Israel as well as other large portions of land around the Mediterranean Sea (Daniel 2:31–45).

Bible prophecy experts often identify these empires as:

1. The Babylonian Empire, led by Nebuchadnezzar himself. It is represented by the golden head of the statue (Daniel 2:37–38).
2. The Medo-Persian Empire which would conquer Babylon. It is represented by the statue's chest and two arms that were made of silver (Daniel 2:32, 2:39). This conquest occurred during Daniel's own lifetime, after Darius the Mede invaded Babylon while its king was throwing a decadent party (Daniel 5:30–31).
3. The Greek Empire, which conquered most of the known world under the leadership of Alexander the Great (Daniel 2:32, 2:39, 8:1–8). It is represented by the statue's lower torso and thighs made of brass.

4. The Roman Empire, which is represented as the two iron legs of the statue (Daniel 2:40). The two iron legs represent how the Roman Empire was eventually split into two semi-independent regions. The Eastern part was centered in Constantinople, and the Western part was centered in Rome.

At the peak of its power, the Roman Empire certainly crushed and conquered the whole known world (Daniel 2:40). At the time, this included large portions of land that are now in southern Europe, as well as Britain, Turkey, Syria, Lebanon, Israel, Egypt, Libya, Algeria, and Morocco, among others.

After discussing the Roman Empire as the two iron legs of the statue, Daniel moves on to talk about the statue's feet and ten toes. Yet these feet are not described as being a fifth kingdom that is separate from Rome. So perhaps the feet and toes are better seen as an extension of Rome's two iron legs, or as a secondary stage of the Roman Empire.

The two feet with ten toes are made of a mix of iron and clay. Therefore, this form of the Roman Empire will be partly strong, but also partly weak, and it will not hold itself together very well (Daniel 2:42–43).

Many end-times prophecy experts believe that the European Union currently fits these criteria. Some of the countries within the EU and the Eurozone are economically strong and are significant players in international politics. Yet other countries within the EU are economically weaker, and are not as influential.

There are disagreements between these countries that lead to tension when the EU's politicians try to make decisions that affect the entire EU. This reality makes some political commentators believe that some countries would be better off leaving the EU and Eurozone, thus making the union somewhat fragile.

The EU currently occupies some of the same land as the ancient Roman Empire did. The EU also includes the land that belonged to the smaller Holy Roman Empire that existed from about 800 to 1800 AD, mostly in what is today Germany, Italy, Switzerland, and parts of France, Poland, Austria, and a few other European countries.

Due to these similarities, some Bible prophecy experts believe that the European Union will be reconfigured into this final "Revived" Roman Empire during the chaos that will follow the Rapture.

The EU may become more influential around the world depending on how many people it loses in the Rapture as compared to the United States of America. It may also depend on which countries will go to war during the Second Seal judgment, and when the Psalm 83 or Gog-Magog wars will occur. More detail on these two specific wars will be discussed in the Appendix of this book.

If other currently-major world powers such as Russia or China experience partial destruction or at least suffer significant military setbacks during the Second Seal judgment or the Gog-Magog War, the EU could rise to become the major superpower left in the world during the Tribulation.

Thus, even if the EU does not literally become a new Roman Empire that conquers the whole world, it could gain a strong influence over all other countries who would look to it for leadership, like how many of the USA's allies and trading partners rely on its leadership today.

There is also the intriguing fact that one symbol used on Europe's money and in some of its government institutions is of a woman named Europa who is sometimes depicted as sitting on a bull. In ancient Greek mythology, this bull was the god Zeus in disguise.

It is therefore interesting that John symbolically describes "Babylon" as a woman who is sitting on the Antichrist's government, which is symbolically described as a terrible seven-headed beast (Revelation 17:1–8). "Babylon" will also have influence over many people of different nations who speak different languages (Revelation 17:15).

Admittedly, this symbol in Revelation is not a perfect match for Europa and the bull. However, the similarity between the two symbolic women both being depicted as sitting on an animal/beast is a potentially interesting hint that the EU may come to be related to the Antichrist and his empire.

If so, then the identification of "Babylon" as the left-behind corrupt remnants of the Roman Catholic Church would fit well with Europe becoming the main seat of the Antichrist's government. Historically, the Roman Catholic Church has had significant power over continental Europe's leaders and people.

On the other hand, other prophecy experts think that the final Revived Roman Empire will actually be a completely global empire.

These prophecy experts envision the world being split into ten regions that would include the EU, as well as a North American Union, an African Union, a South American Union, and so forth. Each of the ten regions will have one single leader, who will be one of the ten "kings" who will rule the world with the Antichrist for a short period of time (Revelation 17:12).

As an alternative interpretation, even today, there are global organizations of countries whose leaders could perhaps become the ten kings that will have worldwide influence during the Tribulation. For example, the G7 would only need three more countries to be added to it to create ten global leaders, to set the end-times political scene for the rise of the Antichrist. There is also the less well-known G-10, which is a group of ten countries who all agreed to work with the

IMF, and the D-10, which is a group of the world's ten leading democracies.

But maybe the ten kings will be a brand-new group of ten world leaders who will emerge only after the Rapture. For example, a former US President claimed that if humanity became convinced that aliens existed and were a threat to the world, it could unite humanity in a way that has never happened before. If the Rapture were falsely explained to the world as being a mass alien abduction, it might rapidly cause the formation of a one-world government with ten leaders.

Regardless of which option will be correct, the Antichrist would then somehow appear as another leader, who will conquer or subdue three of these ten leaders (Daniel 7:8, 7:24). The ten world leaders will later give all their power to the Antichrist (Revelation 13:7–8, 17:12–13).

No matter what form this final empire will actually take, the Bible says it will be destroyed only seven years later.

In Nebuchadnezzar's dream, this last world empire was destroyed by a boulder that smashed into the statue's feet. As a result, the boulder destroyed the entire statue, which can be seen as representing all of humanity's attempts at world domination. Then the boulder became a mountain that filled the whole world (Daniel 2:34–35, 2:44–45). This boulder clearly represents the Millennial Kingdom of Jesus, because

Jesus will destroy the Antichrist and the Antichrist's empire, and then will rule the entire world for at least a thousand years (Revelation 11:15, 20:4–6).

However, to really understand the details of this final world empire that is described in the Book of Daniel and in the Book of Revelation, it is necessary to examine another dream that was given to the prophet Daniel.

Daniel's dream will help interpret the complicated symbol of the beast that comes out of the sea that the Apostle John used to represent the Antichrist and his empire in Revelation chapter 13.

This analysis will provide more clues as to how the Antichrist will gain power over the whole world, and what the Antichrist will do during his reign.

Daniel's Dream Of The Four Beasts

In Daniel's dream, the same four empires that were seen by Nebuchadnezzar in his dream are now represented by unusual animal-like beasts (Daniel 7:1–8).

The first beast was a lion with eagle's wings (Daniel 7:3–4). It corresponds with Babylon, just like how Babylon was identified as the head of the statue in Nebuchadnezzar's dream (Daniel 2:37–38). The Babylonian Empire was famous for its statues and mosaics of winged guardian lions that had human heads, which can be seen in some museums today.

It is thought that how Daniel saw the wings being plucked off this strange lion (Daniel 7:3-4) represents Nebuchadnezzar's humiliation by God, when he lost his mind for a period of time and behaved like a wild animal as divine punishment for his pride (Daniel 4:28-33).

Yet the lion was eventually given a man's mind (Daniel 7:4). This happened when Nebuchadnezzar was restored to sanity after he repented of his pride and acknowledged that only God is God (Daniel 4:34-37).

The second beast that looked like a bear represents the Medo-Persian Empire (Daniel 7:5). This was the second major empire after Babylon to control the land of Israel.

It was powerful and large, but its armies were relatively slow and lumbering, like a bear. It may have also been lopsided in how power was divided between the Medes and Persians within this empire, which is represented as the bear being raised up on one of its sides.

Medo-Persia also conquered three smaller countries (Babylon, Egypt, and Lydia), which are represented as ribs being eaten in the bear's mouth.

The third beast was like a leopard, but with four wings and four heads. This represents the Greek Empire, which conquered the Persians (Daniel 7:6). Alexander the Great conquered a large portion of the known world at the time, and began spreading Greece's culture and language to these regions all around the Mediterranean Sea.

Alexander the Great's army moved quickly, like a leopard. Yet when he died, the empire was split among his four top generals who later fought among themselves, as described in Daniel chapter 11. Thus, the leopard is depicted as having four heads and four wings, representing the Greek empire's eventual fourfold division of both government leadership and military capability (Daniel 7:6, Daniel 8:8, 8:22).

Daniel's fourth beast was described as being terrifying and extremely strong. It had large iron teeth that devoured the world, and its feet trampled whatever was left over (Daniel 7:7–8, 7:24). It was described as having ten horns (Daniel 7:8).

The Roman Empire was unprecedented in power, territory, and duration. It crushed many smaller nations with the effective military power of the Roman legions. This matches well with how Daniel's fourth beast was said to have iron teeth, and it trampled and crushed the whole world, much like the two legs of iron did in Nebuchadnezzar's dream (Daniel 2:40).

Rome slowly conquered the Greek empire a little at a time. Once Rome controlled Israel, it imposed rulers who were under Rome's power. Herod and Pontius Pilate were examples of such rulers during Jesus' time. The people of Israel hated being under Roman rule, and they expected their Messiah to defeat the Romans and return self-governance to Israel (Acts 1:6).

This is what the people thought Jesus would do when he rode into Jerusalem on a donkey, one week before he would be crucified. By riding on a donkey, Jesus fulfilled an Old Testament prophecy and showed he was identifying himself as Israel's rightful king (Matthew 21:1–11, John 12:12–19, Zechariah 9:9–10).

Israel's religious leaders plotted for Jesus to be killed, due to their fear that if Jesus were declared to be Israel's king, the Romans would invade and kill many people in order to put down an insurrection (John 11:47–53). Thus, Pontius Pilate was interested in figuring out if Jesus was Israel's king, but Israel's leadership denied that Jesus was their king (Matthew 27:11–26, John 19:12–16).

Yet as will be seen in Chapter 8, Jesus truly is Israel's true and eternal king, and Jesus will destroy the Revived Roman Empire that will exist during the Tribulation.

However, it is not clear what the ten horns on the fourth beast in Daniel's vision represent. These will make much more sense once Daniel's vision is compared to John's vison of the beast that comes up from the sea in Revelation chapter 13.

THE BEAST THAT COMES FROM THE SEA

In the Book of Revelation chapter 13, John sees a vision of a beast that comes out of the sea.

In the Old Testament, sea monsters were sometimes used to represent foreign oppressors like Egypt or Babylon (e.g. Ezekiel 29:3, Jeremiah 51:34). Both John's beast and Daniel's beasts are depicted as coming out from the sea (Daniel 7:2, Revelation 13:1). The sea was seen by ancient Near-Eastern cultures to be a source of chaos and destruction.

John's beast is described as having a body like a leopard, feet like a bear, and a mouth like a lion (Revelation 13:2). These are all the same animals as in Daniel's dream, but now, parts of the first three beasts are combined into this final unnatural beast.

Daniel never described the body of the fourth beast in his dream, because he only mentioned the teeth and horns (Daniel 7:7–8).

In Daniel's vision, the lion, bear, and leopard each successively lose their power, but their lives are preserved for a while longer. It is only the fourth beast that is fully destroyed by divine fire (Daniel 7:11–12).

Based on John's description of the beast that comes out of the sea, it appears that this fourth empire will contain elements of the previous three empires that continued to live on even after they were defeated. So likewise, elements of these three previous empires

(Babylon, Medo-Persia, and Greece) may have persisted in the Roman Empire, and may exist again in the Revived Roman Empire.

For example, it is well known that Roman culture was significantly influenced by the Greek culture that came before it. Today, many parts of Western democratic countries' culture, law, and government can be seen as being influenced by Ancient Rome.

So, these elements from previous empires that carried over into the Roman Empire will only be fully eliminated from the world once the fourth and last beast is killed at Jesus' Second Coming.

As for the scarlet red color of John's beast (Revelation 17:3), it is the same color as the red dragon that is described in Revelation 12:3. This dragon represents Satan (Revelation 12:3–12), who will give his power and authority to the beast that comes out of the sea (Revelation 13:2–4).

Both the dragon and the beast are represented as having seven heads and ten horns, with ten crowns on their ten horns (Revelation 12:3, 13:1, 17:3).

Daniel explains that the ten horns with ten crowns represent ten leaders/kings (Daniel 7:23–24). John adds that these kings had not yet received power, because they will receive power for only a short time, at the same time as when the Antichrist rules the world (Revelation 17:12).

Some Bible commentators have tried to link the ten horns to ten specific historical Roman emperors. However, there is no agreement on which ones they were, because there were more than only ten Roman emperors. Ten Roman emperors also never ruled together at one time, unlike the four separate heads of the Greek Empire. Later, only two emperors ruled at the same time once the Roman Empire was divided into east and west.

In Nebuchadnezzar's dream, after the two iron legs of Rome, the final stage of the statue was depicted as having feet made of iron and clay, and ten toes (Daniel 2:41–43). These toes are also called kings (Daniel 2:44).

Thus, it is likely that the ten horns on Daniel's fourth beast, and on John's beast that comes out of the sea, are the same rulers that are represented by the ten toes of Nebuchadnezzar's statue, on the two feet made of iron and clay that are an extension of the two iron legs of the Roman Empire.

This shows that although the ancient Roman Empire never had ten leaders, the final Revived Roman Empire will initially have ten leaders/kings.

Although this Revived Roman Empire could begin to take form before the Rapture, it is likely that it will only reach its final ten-king form during the chaos that will happen after the Rapture.

Evidence for this claim comes from how John said that the ten rulers/kings had not yet received power, but when they do, they will only have power for a short time along with the Antichrist (Revelation 17:12).

In the next section, it will become clear how the Antichrist will gain power over the ten kings who will rule this final world empire.

THE RISE OF THE ANTICHRIST

Both the prophet Daniel and the Apostle John said very similar things about the rise of the Antichrist to power, using the symbolism of the horns that wear crowns on the fourth beast, which represents the Revived Roman Empire.

Daniel said that among the initial ten horns who represent the ten kings of the Revived Roman Empire, there will appear another "little" horn. This little horn will somehow replace or uproot three of these initial ten horns/kings (Daniel 7:7–8, 7:20, 7:23–24).

This new horn/king represents the Antichrist, because Daniel says the horn will make war with the saints, but will be defeated by Jesus himself (Daniel 7:20–22, 8:23–25). These details are consistent with John's descriptions of the actions of the beast/Antichrist in Revelation 13:1–8, 17:8–14, and 19:11–20.

Therefore, when the Antichrist first appears on the world scene during the First Seal judgment, he may be victorious because he will have already conquered or overcome three other rulers (Revelation 6:1–2).

The Abomination of Desolation

But what is represented by the seven heads of the beast that comes out of the sea that John describes in Revelation? Why are there ten horns on the beast, but only seven heads?

This is complex, but if this symbolism is deciphered correctly, it gives a major clue as to why the ten kings will give their power to the Antichrist (Revelation 17:12–13), and why the world will be deceived into worshipping the Antichrist as God (Revelation 13:3–8, 2 Thessalonians 2:3–12).

John said that the seven heads of the beast that comes out of the sea represent two different things:

1. Seven mountains that "Babylon" sits on (Revelation 17:9). These mountains are thought to be a reference to the city of Rome that was built on seven large hills (Revelation 17:18).
2. Seven kings (Revelation 17:10).

It should be noted that the seven kings are not related in any way to the seven mountains that "Babylon" sits on, or to the ten kings that will rule at the same time as the Antichrist. Yet the seven heads of the beast are used by John to give clues about both the identity of "Babylon" and the identity of the beast, although in different ways.

For now, the focus will be on how John said the seven heads represent seven kings.

Five of these kings had already fallen from power when John wrote the Book of Revelation. One was currently in power, and another one was not yet in power, but John said that when this king appears, he will have power for only a little while (Revelation 17:10).

One of these seven heads is also described as being mortally wounded, but it is later healed, causing the entire world to marvel at it (Revelation 13:3).

Given these details, who are these seven kings/heads?

Some Bible commentators try to claim that these kings were ancient Roman emperors, but if so, it is difficult to choose which of the emperors should be counted, because there were more than only seven emperors.

Similarly, some Bible commentators try to claim that the head that was mortally wounded with a sword but lived represents Nero. Emperor Nero committed suicide several decades before John wrote the Book of Revelation, although there may have been a myth that Nero would come back to life and regain power over the Roman Empire with the help of the Parthians. This is called the *Nero Redivivus Legend.*

The Bible says the number 666 will be the number of the man who will become the Antichrist, but no instruction is given on how this number should be calculated (Revelation 13:18).

Gematria refers to ancient methods of assigning numbers to the letters of a word, and then using the numbers of all the letters in the word to calculate a final number that was thought to represent something significant about the word in question. Some prophecy interpreters believe that Emperor Nero's name and title can be converted into the number 666 using Hebrew *gematria.*

However, Nero obviously did not come back to life. Also, although Nero persecuted Christians in the city of Rome, he did not mandate empire-wide persecution of Christians. He also did not demand that everyone worship him or an image of him, nor take his Mark in/on their foreheads or right hands in order to be able to buy or sell (Revelation 13:14–18).

Therefore, a different interpretation of the beast's head that is wounded by a sword but lived seems to be necessary.

As in Daniel's dream of the beasts, it seems there is a precedent for using the multiple heads of the beasts to represent divisions of leadership. Recall how the four heads of the leopard-like beast represented how the Greek Empire was divided among four leaders after Alexander the Great's death (Daniel 7:6).

Yet John specifies that this division among the seven heads of his beast is chronological, not regional (Revelation 17:10).

There is much debate among Biblical interpreters what the seven heads of John's beast represent. One of the most convincing interpretations again makes use of Daniel's dream.

If the body of John's beast is described as having parts from the three empires that came before it, then perhaps three of the beast's heads can also represent these same historical empires.

Another head would be the Roman Empire that was currently ruling when John was alive, and the next would be a yet-future empire, such as the Revived Roman Empire.

But then two heads out of seven are still not identified. If the heads represent empires, then perhaps John is looking backward in time to also include empires that were even older than Babylon, such as Egypt and Assyria, that were not included in Daniel's dream.

An ancient commentator on the Book of Revelation named Andrew of Caesarea took this position. In chronological order, he suggested that the seven heads of John's beast could represent the empires of:

1. Egypt.

2. Assyria.
3. Babylon, represented as Daniel's first lion-like beast, and the head of gold on Nebuchadnezzar's statue.
4. Medo-Persia, represented as Daniel's second bear-like beast, and the chest/arms of silver on the statue.
5. Greece, represented as Daniel's third leopard-like beast, and the torso/hips of bronze on the statue.
6. Rome, represented as Daniel's fourth beast, and the two iron legs of the statue. It was currently ruling during John's lifetime.
7. The Revived Roman Empire, which will appear again during the Tribulation. It is represented as the ten horns on Daniel's fourth beast, and the feet of iron/clay with ten toes on the statue.

All of these six historical empires have ruled over the land of Israel, and all of them have persecuted or fought against God's people (i.e., Israelites, Jews, or Christians). The same will be true for the Revived Roman Empire, during the Tribulation (Revelation 13:7–8).

Thus, some commentators argue that the head that is mortally wounded by the sword but still lived is describing how the ancient Roman Empire disappeared from the world, but will appear again as the Revived Roman Empire during the Tribulation.

In this interpretation, the Antichrist would then be the "eighth" king that John saw, who was initially part of the seventh head (i.e., the Revived Roman Empire).

Thus, it seems the Antichrist will initially appear as a "little horn" that replaces three of the ten horns on the seventh head of the beast (Daniel 7:8). But the Antichrist will grow in power until he eventually controls the entire beast (Revelation 17:11–13).

Bible interpreters often claim that the world will marvel at the reappearance of the Revived Roman Empire, and will worship the dragon (a.k.a., Satan) who gives this empire his authority. Everyone will wonder who can fight against this beast/empire (Revelation 13:3–4). However, it does not completely make sense why the whole world would marvel at and worship an empire.

Also, the False Prophet does not make the whole world worship an empire, but instead makes the world worship a particular man. This will be done by making an idol of this man that can appear to speak, and by requiring everyone to take a "Mark" that is associated with the number of a man that equals 666 (Revelation 13:12–18).

Furthermore, the Book of Revelation seems to use the beast's actions to describe the Antichrist himself, once he receives the full power of the other ten kings (Revelation 17:12–13). After all, the beast is described as doing things are best seen as the actions of a single person, rather than of an entire empire.

For example, the beast will kill the Two Witnesses (Revelation 11:7), blaspheme God (Revelation 13:5), be wounded by a sword but still live (Revelation 13:14), and be captured at the battle of Armageddon (Revelation 19:19–20). The False Prophet will also do miracles in the presence of the beast (Revelation 13:14), implying that there may be times when he will not be in the beast's personal presence, and so be unable to do miracles.

Insight into this question of how the beast seems to be describing both an empire and the leader of the empire may be found by returning to Daniel's dream of the four beasts. There, the actions of Daniel's first lion-like beast that represented the Babylonian Empire seem to correspond to the events of Nebuchadnezzar's personal life. It tells about how he went insane as a divine judgment for his pride, but he later regained his sanity (Daniel 7:3–4, Daniel 4:28–35).

So it could be that all of these four empires were so totalitarian that whatever their leader did, the entire empire could be seen as doing.

Therefore, the seventh head of John's beast may actually represent the Antichrist himself, once he becomes the supreme ruler of the entire Revived Roman Empire. Then, the Antichrist and his Revived Roman

Empire will be the seventh head of the chronological "beast" of totalitarian human empires.

In this case, then, the seventh head of John's beast that is wounded but lives could actually indicate that it will be the Antichrist *himself* who receives what should be a deadly wound from a sword, but somehow the wound will be healed, and he will survive (Revelation 13:3–4, 13:12).

Some prophecy experts argue that the Antichrist's recovery from what should have been a deadly wound will appear to be so stunning that it could even seem to everyone that the Antichrist *did* die, and actually came back to life! In this way, the Antichrist will be the ultimate false Christ, who will try to duplicate Jesus' miraculous resurrection. Yet it will probably only be an impressive deception (2 Thessalonians 2:9–12).

The whole world will be so amazed by this apparent miracle that they will worship the Antichrist as if he were divine. Everyone will wonder how anyone can defeat him, because he will seem to be indestructible (Revelation 13:3–4).

This interpretation seems much easier to imagine than the alternative claim that the world will worship a revived Roman Empire. It is also much easier to create an idol of a person than of an entire empire (Revelation 13:14–15).

So it seems that after the Antichrist's near-miraculous recovery from being wounded by a sword, the ten rulers/kings of the Revived Roman Empire will give all their power to the Antichrist. He will become the most powerful person on the planet, although these ten rulers/kings seem to stay on as sub-rulers who cooperate with the Antichrist and help him administer his worldwide empire (Revelation 17:12–13,17:17, 13:7–8).

At that time, the Antichrist effectively becomes "the beast," and so he is referred to in this way throughout the rest of the Book of Revelation, because whatever he says is what his entire empire will do.

This symbolism makes sense, because then, the Antichrist will not only be the seventh head of the beast that will be wounded and return to life, but he will also personify the worst traits of all seven previous totalitarian empires. Yet the Antichrist will outdo them all by conquering the entire planet, and demanding the worship of everyone, everywhere.

Many of the leaders of these historical empires also blasphemously thought themselves to be gods, or others thought that these leaders were gods or had become gods (e.g., the Egyptian pharaohs, Nebuchadnezzar, Alexander the Great, and the Roman emperors). The Antichrist will become the ultimate example of this pattern (Revelation 13:5) when he will declare himself to be God in the rebuilt Temple in Jerusalem (2 Thessalonians 2:3–4).

Thus, in summary, the Antichrist initially appears as just a little horn/leader that replaces three of the other ten horns/leaders on the seventh head of the beast, which is the Revived Roman Empire. Once these ten leaders give him all their power, the Antichrist becomes the seventh king/head of the beast that "was," then "was not" because he dies, and then rises from the "abyss" (i.e., death/hell) in an apparent resurrection. He then becomes the "eighth" king, that is also the entire beast, which will finally be destroyed at Jesus' Second Coming (Revelation 17:8, 13:3).

Some Bible prophecy experts even argue that after the Antichrist's death and pseudo-resurrection, he will become possessed by Satan himself. This will make the Antichrist become the "son of perdition" (2 Thessalonians 2:3).

During Jesus' First Coming, his disciple Judas Iscariot was also called the son of perdition, who was doomed to be lost once he became possessed by Satan and betrayed Jesus (John 13:27, 17:12). A few prophecy experts see this connection, and so they claim that the Antichrist actually will be Judas Iscariot reincarnated.

This is impossible, though, because people generally only die once, and then face God's judgment (Hebrews 9:27). The only exceptions to this rule were a few people who had recently died and were temporarily brought back to life as a demonstration of God's power over death (e.g., 1 Kings 17:17–24, Mark 5:35–43, Luke 7:11–17, Acts 20:7–12). Yet, unlike the Christians who will be resurrected in glorified, immortal, perfect bodies at the Rapture, these people would have been raised back to life in their regular mortal bodies, and so they would have died again sometime later.

Therefore, it is highly unlikely that God would resurrect Judas after his body has been decomposed for nearly two thousand years, only so that he could become the Antichrist. Furthermore, Judas was Jewish, not Roman. As seen earlier, the Antichrist is prophesied to come from the people who destroyed the second Temple in Jerusalem, who were the Romans (Daniel 9:26–27).

It makes much more sense to interpret the reference to the Antichrist being the "son of perdition" as simply meaning that the Antichrist will become possessed by Satan, just like Judas was possessed by Satan when he betrayed Jesus.

The Bible shows that Satan wants to be worshipped as God (Matthew 4:8–10), and to take over God's throne (Isaiah 14:12–17). By possessing the Antichrist and ruling the entire world, while also being worshipped by most people on the planet, Satan will come as close as possible to achieving his objective.

The incident when the Antichrist will appear to die and come back to life will likely occur before the Antichrist will declare himself to be God in the rebuilt Temple in Jerusalem (2 Thessalonians 2:3–4, Revelation 13:5–6). It is only after such a miraculous pseudo-resurrection that such a claim to divinity would appear plausible to the people of the world.

The Antichrist's declaration that he is God in the Temple will desecrate the Temple, and thereby stop the sacrifices that will have been going on there during the first half of the Tribulation (Daniel 9:26–27, 8:9–14). This event is referred to as the *Abomination of Desolation*.

Something very similar to this happened once before, when the Seleucid king Antiochus Epiphanes tried to prohibit many traditional Jewish practices during his reign from 215 BC to 164 BC. He even sacrificed a pig on the altar of the Temple in Jerusalem, which desecrated it. This caused a Jewish revolt, which led Antiochus to kill many people in Israel. It is described in the Book of 2 Maccabees that is part of the Biblical apocrypha. The re-dedication of the Temple after its desecration by Antiochus is now celebrated annually by Jews during the feast of Hanukkah.

Daniel prophesied that all of this would occur, and that Antiochus would have delusions of being a deity (Daniel 11:36–39). *Epiphanes* even translates to "God manifest," or "God revealed," which shows just how arrogant Antiochus was to call himself this name. As a play on words, his critics called him Antiochus *Epimanes*, meaning "the mad one."

However, Jesus warned that another Abomination of Desolation would happen at some point in the future. Antiochus Epiphanes is therefore seen as a *type* of the Antichrist, because he acted in a way that foreshadowed what the Antichrist will do.

Jesus warned that when anyone who is living in the portion of Israel called Judea sees this Abomination of Desolation happen, they should immediately flee to the mountains, without stopping to pack any supplies or even pick up their coats, or they will lose their lives (Matthew 24:15–18, Mark 13:14–16, Luke 17:31–35).

From this point in time, the Antichrist will rule the world for forty-two months until he will be thrown into the Lake of Fire at Jesus' Second Coming (Revelation 13:5, 19:19–20).

It will also likely be just after the Abomination of Desolation when the Antichrist and the ten kings will turn against "Babylon," which formerly had some level of control over the Revived Roman Empire (Revelation 17:16–17).

"Babylon" will be destroyed within a single day, and even a single hour (Revelation 18:7–10, 18:17–19). It seems that the destruction of "Babylon" will cause economic distress around the world, because the merchants of the world will mourn that no one will buy their luxury goods anymore (Revelation 18:11–20).

Due to the negative reaction of the world's merchants, perhaps the destruction of "Babylon" will occur at the same time as the implementation of the Mark of the Beast, because no one will be able to buy or sell without this Mark (Revelation 13:16–17).

If so, then after the destruction of "Babylon," the Mark of the Beast system would be the only remaining economic system for all trade and commerce during the rest of the Tribulation.

Although "Babylon" has been discussed earlier, now is the time to look more in depth at the symbols used to describe it, to identify it in more detail.

The Destruction of "Babylon"

There is much debate among Bible prophecy experts regarding what the Book of Revelation symbolically represents as the blasphemous prostitute named "Babylon," who is depicted as sitting on the Antichrist's "beast" government.

Whatever "Babylon" is, it seems it represents something that is associated with worldwide idolatry and immorality. This immorality will be participated in by government leaders as well as most other people (Revelation 17:1–2). "Babylon" will likely have come to dominate the world during the first half of the Tribulation.

"Babylon" is related in some way to a city that is built on seven mountains (Revelation 17:9, 17:18). This is usually thought to be Rome, as this was the most famous city that was built on seven hills during the time when John was writing the Book of Revelation. However, "Babylon" will also influence people all around the world, which are represented as "many waters" (Revelation 17:2).

"Babylon" will be associated with the colors of purple and scarlet (red), and it will initially have great wealth and influence over the ten world rulers and the Antichrist (Revelation 17:3–4).

Some prophecy experts identify the colors of purple and scarlet, and the great wealth as indicating that "Babylon" will be formed from the corrupt and apostate remnants of Roman Catholicism that will be left behind after the Rapture.

Currently, Roman Catholicism is the only major world religion whose leaders wear robes in these colors, and which is also incredibly rich.

Roman Catholicism's headquarters are also located in Vatican City, which is within the city of Rome. Rome has been called the City of Seven Hills because of its geography.

The Vatican even has its own "bank" (The Institute for the Works of Religion) that handles the Roman Catholic Church's financial investments.

"Babylon" will also persecute and kill some of the Christians who convert after the Rapture, because "Babylon" is depicted as being drunk on the blood of the saints (Revelation 17:5–6, 18:24).

In John's time, Rome was simultaneously an empire, a city, and a system of government with an idolatrous religion that persecuted and killed Christians. Therefore, many Bible commentators believe that John was using "Babylon" as a code word to talk about the historical Roman Empire, which was then persecuting Christians.

However, the historical Roman Empire was not destroyed by a powerful leader with ten sub-leaders in a day or an hour, as John says will happen for "Babylon" (Revelation 18:8–10, 17:16–17). Instead, Emperor Constantine legalized Christianity, and allowed Christian leaders to gain great influence in the Empire.

When the city of Rome fell to barbarians, it was the Roman Catholic Church that remained in place as a stable form of local government for the regions that formerly composed the western half of the Roman Empire.

Popes and church leaders became powerful political figures. Unfortunately, these positions were sometimes given to unscrupulous men who paid large sums of money for them, or who used other unethical means of obtaining power.

Some popes used their power to persuade people to go on crusades where the people committed many awful deeds under the church's sanction. Later, the Roman Catholic Church gained significant power over emperors during the formation of the Holy Roman Empire.

In the past, the Roman Catholic Church has also persecuted people of many different religions. One might think of various historical inquisitions and wars against other groups of Christians who did not agree with official Catholic doctrines.

The Roman Catholic Church also persecuted Christians who translated the Bible into their own languages, or who broke off to form their own churches during the Reformation. Some examples of Christians that were martyred for this include Jan Hus, possibly considered to be the first Reformer, and the followers of John Wycliffe who were called Lollards.

All of these historical facts make it seem that "Babylon" in the Book of Revelation is most likely the corrupted remnants of the Roman Catholic Church that will be left behind after the Rapture.

Currently, the Roman Catholic Church is the largest denomination of Christianity, which is the largest religion on the planet. Yet the Roman Catholic Church is also likely to consist of many people who are unsaved. This is because it is easy for people to mistakenly put their trust in the Roman Catholic

Church's authority, traditions, and rituals, rather than trusting Jesus and his death on the cross for forgiveness of their sins.

These unsaved people will be left behind at the Rapture, but they will still believe they are Christians because they attended a church or participated in various rituals, yet without ever having had personal faith in Jesus Christ as their Savior. Tragically, even some of the Roman Catholic Church's priests, bishops, cardinals, and other leaders may not be true believers in Jesus.

Catholics today who are true believers in Jesus are often frustrated and saddened by the immoral activities of some of their clergy, and the corruption that is exposed within their church. Even some Catholic theologians have criticized some questionable statements that have been made by their leaders.

All of this means that the Roman Catholic Church's power structure will likely remain at least partly intact after the Rapture. In comparison, other Christian denominations will likely lose larger numbers of both lay members and clergy when the Rapture occurs.

Therefore, some remnants of Orthodox or Protestant denominations that will be left behind after the Rapture may quickly decide to merge with the Roman Catholic Church. Even today, there are individuals who are calling on Protestants and Orthodox Christians to reunite with Roman Catholicism, which they say is the one true church.

In recent years, the Roman Catholic Church's leadership has also shown interest in reaching out to try to find common ground with other monotheistic religions like Islam and Judaism.

However, in order for Christians to find theological agreement with these other religions, several major Christian doctrines such as the uniqueness of Jesus Christ, the significance of his death and resurrection, and the importance of believing in Jesus alone for eternal salvation have to all be minimized or ignored.

Instead of speaking of Jesus or the Trinity, many of these ecumenical agreements only have vague mentions of "God." In this way, it can be incorrectly claimed that Christians, Jews, and Muslims all worship the same God, because they all trace their history back to Abraham.

For example, the Abrahamic Family House that has recently opened in Abu Dhabi contains a worship facility for each of these three religions. Likewise, the House of One that is being built in Berlin, Germany, advertises itself to be a house of prayer for all three of the world's major monotheistic religions (Christianity, Judaism, and Islam).

Thus, perhaps early on in the Tribulation, these three religions will come together under the leadership of the Roman Catholic Church to form "Babylon," and together, they will begin to once again persecute true Christians (Revelation 6:9–11).

However, Christians who refuse to join this new world religion will refuse to give up their belief that faith in Christ is the only way to have eternal life (John 3:16). Because of this belief, these true Christians will likely be called intolerant and hateful. They will be seen as worthy of being persecuted and even killed for committing the offensive blasphemy of saying that only Jesus is Lord (1 Corinthians 8:6, 12:3), and for claiming that there is no one else besides Jesus who can eternally save people (Acts 4:12).

So these true Christians who have been persecuted by "Babylon" will celebrate when it is finally destroyed by the Antichrist and the ten kings (Revelation 18:20).

In addition to destroying "Babylon," the Antichrist will also kill the Two Witnesses in Jerusalem, 1,260 days after the witnesses first began prophesying (Revelation 11:1–13).

This execution will probably occur around the same half-way point of the Tribulation as when the Abomination of Desolation happens. This is when the Antichrist will declare himself to be God in the rebuilt Temple in Jerusalem, thus causing the sacrifices to stop and the Temple to become 'desolate' (Daniel 9:27, 8:13).

At that point, with "Babylon" destroyed and the Two Witnesses dead, the Antichrist will have no one left who will oppose him, except for those people who became Christians after the Rapture.

Although these saints will have been persecuted severely during the Fifth Seal judgment when many of them were killed, now the Antichrist will make war against them and overcome most of them (Revelation 13:7).

This extreme persecution of any remaining Christians will happen after the faithful remnants of Israel escape into the wilderness during the Abomination of Desolation. These remnants of faithful Israel will be protected there for the rest of the Tribulation, which is another 1,260 days, or forty-two months (Revelation 12:14–17, 13:5, Daniel 12:7).

At that point in time, the Antichrist will have destroyed all other religious figures who could compete with him. He will have claimed to have come back to life, and to actually be God.

The only religious leader left who will have any power will be the False Prophet, who will support and endorse the Antichrist's claim to be God. The False Prophet will be discussed more in the next chapter.

Chapter 6

The False Prophet and the Image of the Beast

Similar to the warnings about many "antichrists" who will deceive many people by claiming to be the Messiah, Jesus also warned about false prophets who would come in the last days (Matthew 24:11).

A prophet is a person who speaks to others on God's behalf, to give them messages from God. This does not always mean they make predictions about what will happen in the future, although this can be part of a prophet's message, if God wants people to know what will happen ahead of time (e.g. John 14:29, Matthew 24:24–25).

False prophets have always been a problem for God's people. They claim to speak on God's behalf, but they are actually liars. In the last days, some false prophets will even teach things that are sinful, heretical, and demonic, because the false prophets will be influenced by evil spirits (1 Timothy 4:1-3, 2 Peter 2:1-3).

So, just as the Antichrist will be the ultimate example of all antichrists that came before, who falsely portrayed themselves to be the Messiah, the False Prophet will be the ultimate example of a person who will claim to speak for God, but who will actually be lying.

The Bible does not say exactly when the False Prophet will appear on the world scene during the Tribulation.

The clearest mention of him is in Revelation 19:20. Here, he is identified as someone who did miracles to deceive those who received the Mark of the Beast and worshiped the Image of the Beast. Based on this identification, it is clear that the False Prophet is also described in Revelation 13:11-18.

In Revelation chapter 13, the Antichrist and his empire are symbolized as the first beast, the one that comes out of the sea, with seven heads and ten horns. The False Prophet is represented as a second beast who rises out of the land. This beast has two horns, and it is described as looking like a lamb but speaking like a dragon (Revelation 13:11).

Most end-times prophecy experts believe that the False Prophet will be a very influential religious figure. He will initially seem to be a good person, gentle and harmless, like a lamb. But the things the False Prophet says will sound like they come from Satan. Satan is represented as a dragon throughout the Book of Revelation (Revelation 12:9).

Jesus is referred to as the Lamb of God who was sacrificed for the sins of the world (John 1:29, Revelation 5:6). So maybe the False Prophet will appear to impersonate Jesus in some ways.

Many Bible prophecy experts suspect that whoever will be the Roman Catholic Pope during the Tribulation could be a good candidate for the False Prophet.

The Pope is sometimes referred to as the "Vicar of Christ," because the Pope should attempt to be Jesus Christ's most influential representative to the world, and also the most Christ-like person in the Roman Catholic Church.

If the Pope were to endorse the Antichrist as being God, especially after the Antichrist's apparently-miraculous recovery after being mortally wounded with a sword (Revelation 13:3, 13:12), many people would likely believe him.

If the False Prophet were the Pope, it would also fit well with the suggestion that the false religion that is depicted as a blasphemous woman sitting on the beast is the left-behind and corrupted remains of Roman Catholicism (Revelation 17:3–5).

Regardless of whether this identification is correct, the second beast, a.k.a. the False Prophet, will do several notable things that will make it clear who he is when he appears.

First, the False Prophet will be able to do impressive but deceptive miracles when he is in the presence of the Antichrist, including making fire come down from the sky (Revelation 13:13–14).

This action will appear to duplicate the miracle done by one of the most powerful Old-Testament prophets named Elijah, when he called down God's fire from Heaven as proof that God was truly God, unlike the false god of other false prophets (1 Kings 18:20–39). This miracle may be another reason the world will be deceived into thinking that the Antichrist really is God.

The False Prophet is also the one who seems to be primarily responsible for convincing the world to worship the Antichrist in two important ways:

1. By instigating the creation of the Image of the Beast/Antichrist. This image will be able to speak, and it will also kill everyone who will not worship it (Revelation 13:14–15).
2. By requiring everyone to take the Mark of the Beast in order to buy or sell (Revelation 13:16–18).

The first point will be discussed in this chapter, while the second is discussed in the next chapter.

THE IMAGE OF THE BEAST

The False Prophet will be the one who will tell the world to make an Image of the Antichrist. This will happen after the Antichrist has been wounded by a sword and then been miraculously healed, or he might even appear to have died and come back to life (Revelation 13:14).

Therefore, the Image of the Beast appears to be a return to idolatry.

In many times in the past, people worshipped statues made of wood, stone, or metal that they thought represented their gods. However, the people were actually worshipping demons (1 Corinthians 10:19–21, Deuteronomy 32:17, Psalm 96:5).

The Bible warns God's people many times to avoid idolatry, which is a sin, because only God should be worshipped (e.g., Acts 21:25, Exodus 20:2–6, Leviticus 26:1, 1 Corinthians 10:14, Matthew 4:10).

There have also been times in the past when world leaders required their people to worship statues that were made to resemble the leader. The most notable instance of this that was recorded in the Bible was done by the Babylonian King Nebuchadnezzar.

King Nebuchadnezzar created a golden statue that was sixty cubits tall (about 100 feet, or 30 meters), and six cubits wide (about 10 feet, or 3 meters). He then gathered all his government officials, and demanded that they bow down and worship this statue when six instruments were played (Daniel 3:1-7).

Whoever refused to worship the statue would be rounded up and thrown into a flaming furnace. This happened to three of the prophet Daniel's friends, but they were miraculously protected because of their faith in God (Daniel 3:8-30).

There are interesting similarities between this incident and the Image of the Beast, and how everyone who refuses to worship it will be killed (Revelation 13:15).

The numbers sixty (cubits tall), six (cubits wide), and six (instruments) appear here in Daniel chapter 3. The Mark of the Beast will be associated with the number 666, which is the "number" of the beast/Antichrist (Revelation 13:18).

In the Bible, certain numbers are associated with particular ideas. For example, seven is the number of divine perfection. Yet the number six is associated with sinful humanity, which falls short of God's divinity and perfection.

The number six also shows up in a very interesting event in the Old Testament that also connects to the number 666.

The giant Goliath was described as being six cubits tall, carrying a spear that weighed six hundred shekels, and he wore or used six pieces of equipment:

a helmet, chainmail coat, two pieces of armor on his legs, a javelin, and a shield (1 Samuel 17:1-7).

Goliath was a fearsome adversary who threatened God's people, but he was killed by the young shepherd David, who would become Israel's best king (1 Samuel 17:41-54). Jesus is described as being the descendant of David who will rule on David's throne forever (2 Samuel 7:12-16, Psalm 110:1-7, Revelation 22:16).

So it is fitting that the Antichrist will be identified with the number 666, and he will be defeated by Jesus, who is called *the* good shepherd, at Jesus' Second Coming (Revelation 19:11-20, John 10:11-15).

Other Bible commentators see similarities between the Image of the Beast, and how some Roman emperors required some of their subjects to offer a sacrifice to statues of the emperor. The Roman emperors were not always thought to be divine during their lives. Some later emperors did portray themselves as being gods even while they were alive.

Once people had made a sacrifice to the statue of the Emperor as a show of loyalty, these people would receive a slip of paper that confirmed they had done so. Some Christians attempted to purchase or forge the slips of paper without offering the sacrifice, but this fraudulent activity was looked down on by other Christians.

In these ways, the Image of the Beast will be a repetition of these past instances of forced idolatry. Yet this time, the idol will be even more deceptive because the idol itself will be able to speak, and seem like it is alive, which past idols never did (Revelation 13:15, Jeremiah 10:14).

Also, the idol itself will be what kills the people who are brought to worship it but refuse to do so. At least some of these people who refuse to worship the Antichrist's Image will be beheaded (Revelation 20:4).

Therefore, some end-times experts suggest that the Image of the Beast might be created using some sort of advanced robotics or AI technology. Some Christian movies based on the Book of Revelation thought that virtual reality could also be part of the Image of the Beast.

It is difficult to say exactly what the Image of the Beast will be, but as with all of these end-times prophecies, the people who are on Earth during the Tribulation will be able to clearly identify it, based on these clues given in the Bible.

The Mark of the Beast will also be clearly identifiable by the people who will be alive at that time, because the Mark has several notable features. This will be the topic of the next chapter.

Chapter 7

The Mark of the Beast

Despite all the judgments and disasters that will occur during the Tribulation, it will be something man-made that is actually the most dangerous to the people who are alive at that time.

Regardless of how many disasters people will survive, it will not matter unless they avoid one very critical thing. It is called the Mark of the Beast, and it is described in Revelation chapter 13.

The identifying features of the Mark of the Beast are:

1. It will be located *in* and/or *on* the skin of a person's forehead or right hand (Revelation 13:16).
2. It is somehow associated with the number 666, which is the number of a person (Revelation

13:18), probably the Antichrist, who is also called "the beast."
3. No one in the entire world, regardless of personal wealth or social status, will be able to buy or sell without taking the Mark of the Beast (Revelation 13:16–17).
4. Anyone who takes the Mark of the Beast will experience God's wrath in the form of being tormented by fire and sulfur, possibly for all eternity (Revelation 14:9–11).

However, the Mark of the Beast will not actually be implemented by the Antichrist himself. Instead, it will be the False Prophet, the man who will do great miracles for the Antichrist, who will demand that everyone take the Mark of the Beast (Revelation 13:11–17).

There has been much speculation over the years about what the Mark of the Beast will actually be, and what technology will be needed to implement it on a worldwide scale.

What Technology Will The Mark of the Beast Use?

Some prophecy experts in the past claimed that the Mark of the Beast could be something as simple as a tattoo, perhaps of an individualized bar code or a QR code. Then, the Antichrist would make laws that demand that the Mark must be shown whenever someone wants to perform a financial transaction.

However, it seems that what the Book of Revelation is describing will be much more serious than this.

If the Mark of the Beast were something that was only expected to be shown before buying or selling using traditional money, there would be resisters who would find ways to get around it. Some resisters might bribe officials to ignore their lack of the Mark, or others might find ways to fake or forge the Mark.

Furthermore, there would be the chance that some people who will take the Mark would feel sympathy for others who will refuse to take the Mark. If these sympathetic individuals were in a position to do so, they could choose to break the law and ignore the need for people to show the Mark to buy or sell, and process their transactions anyway.

This is why many prophecy experts have argued that the Mark of the Beast will be part of a worldwide digital system that will control all financial transactions for everyone on the planet. There would be no way to bypass it

A digital currency would likely be part of this system, along with digital personal identification for each individual who would opt into this system. Once there is no other way to buy or sell except through digital transactions, then access to this digital system could be limited by whether a person has the Mark of the Beast or not.

Therefore, Bible prophecy experts pay close attention to technological developments in the areas of digital currencies, digital identification systems, electronic payment methods, cryptocurrencies, and so forth.

Many prophecy experts are particularly alarmed by advancements made in the last decade or so regarding implantable microchips that could go just under the skin of a person's hand or forehead. These chips could operate using the same sort of technology as is currently used in various contactless forms of payment, such as credit cards.

Microchips of this sort are commonly used in pets to link the pet to a database, so that the pet can be returned to an owner if it is lost, and to help identify it on other veterinary or shelter records.

Occasionally, news stories are published about some companies who have developed these implantable chips for use in various applications, such as to allow people to open doors to their smart vehicles or homes. Other companies use these implanted chips to allow employees to access secured locations, or even just as a convenient way for employees to buy things from the office cafeteria.

Eventually, prophecy experts fear that such microchips might become a mandatory form of digital identification for all people, or become required in order to access digital currencies or perform financial transactions.

As these systems become more developed and are more widely used by people around the world, eventually, there will come a time during the Tribulation when using this sort of digital financial system and the Mark of the Beast will be the only way for anyone to buy or sell.

In this way, the Antichrist and False Prophet would be able to monitor and control everyone in the world, by deciding who is allowed to buy or sell. They may even control exactly what products and services individuals are allowed to buy or sell, or what sorts of jobs individuals are allowed to work at, depending on the individual's personal loyalty or behavior.

Already, some countries are experimenting with digital control systems very much like this, as a way to manipulate the values and behavior of their populations. If individuals do not behave how their government desires, these individuals lose the ability to travel, to use public transit, to attend certain schools, to hold certain jobs or positions in government, or even live in certain forms of housing.

Thus, it does not seem that any further advances in technology are necessary before something like the Mark of the Beast could be created. The only thing holding it back is how currently, most people would not want to opt into such a controlling system if they could avoid it.

Therefore, perhaps the digital control system that will enable the Mark of the Beast will become functional after the Third Seal judgment, when hyperinflation and/or famine become so severe worldwide that people will work for a whole day just to earn enough money to buy a small amount of wheat or barley, to feed themselves and their families (Revelation 6:5–6).

During this Third Seal judgment, the world's leaders, under the guidance of the Antichrist and False Prophet, could decide to try to solve the problem by setting up a brand new economic system. The people of the world will likely be desperate for their leaders to do something, and most people will enthusiastically opt into the new system just to survive.

Something like this has been seen before, during the terrible seven years of famine experienced by Egypt, during the time of Joseph. Back then, Joseph, who had become second-in-command of all Egypt, offered to sell grain that the government had stored up ahead of time to the people who were starving (Genesis 41:25–57).

But eventually, the people ran out of money, and so they traded in all their property and possessions to the government in exchange for grain. Finally, the people sold themselves into slavery to the government in exchange for food (Genesis 47:13–26).

Perhaps this new economic system that the Antichrist and False Prophet will create will be based on a new global digital currency, or maybe carbon credits. This new system could provide a basic income or act like digital ration cards so that everyone will be able to survive. Or maybe it could act like some sort of worldwide economic reset and debt relief for indebted individuals and even for national governments.

But whatever final form the system will take, the Bible says that eventually, no one will be able to avoid taking the Mark of the Beast if they want to buy and sell in this new global digital economic system.

This will be true even if some people who take the Mark might be sympathetic to others who will choose to reject the Mark.

When Will the Mark of the Beast Be Implemented?

It is not clear at what point during the Tribulation the Mark of the Beast will be rolled out. Many prophecy experts suspect that the latest it might be implemented would be just after the Antichrist survives what should have been a deadly sword wound to his head, and he may even appear to die and come back to life (Revelation 13:3, 13:12).

This apparent miracle will convince the world to worship the Antichrist and Satan (Revelation 13:3–4). Therefore, this faux miracle will probably occur shortly before the Antichrist declares himself to be God in the rebuilt Temple in Jerusalem (2 Thessalonians 2:3–4).

Then, the False Prophet will demand that everyone worship the Antichrist. The Image of the Beast will be created to assist with this worship, and it will kill all the people who are brought to it that refuse to worship it (Revelation 13:15). The Bible suggests that the main method of execution for those people who refuse to perform such worship will be beheading (Revelation 20:4).

The Mark of the Beast will help enforce the worship of the Antichrist, because everyone who refuses to take the Mark will be cut off from the world's digital economic system. Thus, there will be very strong motivation for people to take the Mark and worship the Antichrist as God.

Yet somehow, the Bible is clear that some people will survive through the Tribulation without taking the Mark of the Beast or worshiping the Antichrist or his Image. This is because God's penalty for anyone who takes the Mark of the Beast appears to be eternal torment (Revelation 14:9–11). Therefore, it does not seem that anyone who takes the Mark could gain God's approval to survive the Sheep and Goats judgment that will occur after Jesus' Second Coming (Matthew 25:31–46).

As was discussed earlier in Chapter 2, enough people will receive a favorable judgment from Jesus that the world will be repopulated during Jesus' Millennial Kingdom. So presumably, it will be only those people who refuse the Mark of the Beast who will have any chance to pass Jesus' judgment and enter his Millennial Kingdom.

Even then, it will be only those people who refused the Mark of the Beast *and* who provided generously for others who were also in need who will be the ones to earn Jesus' approval. They will gain permission to enter Jesus' kingdom (Matthew 25:34–40).

The Bible does not say how these people will be able to survive and provide generously for others without taking the Mark of the Beast. Perhaps they will have to flee to remote areas in the wilderness and live off the land or forage for food. Or, perhaps there will be some sort of underground barter economy that people without the Mark of the Beast could set up or participate in.

It also seems theoretically possible that some sympathetic people who will take the Mark of the Beast might shelter and provide for their friends, family, and/or neighbors who do not take the Mark. However, if this were the case, then it is unclear why these generous and caring people who helped others survive would not be welcomed into Jesus' Millennial Kingdom.

It seems that Jesus should be pleased with these people's selfless generosity, even though these people took the Mark of the Beast. Yet God's judgment is always righteous, and God does not punish innocent people along with those who are wicked (Genesis 18:25).

God warns that anyone who takes the Mark of the Beast will be tormented with fire and sulfur while in God's own presence, and there will not be any break from this torment for as long as it continues (Revelation 14:9–11). The length of this torment is unclear, but most Bible commentators interpret it as eternal torment in the Lake of Fire, because the Bible says that the "smoke" of these people's torment goes up forever (Revelation 14:11, Revelation 20:14–15).

At Jesus' Second Coming, the Antichrist and the False Prophet will be thrown into the Lake of Fire. These two individuals will suffer forever (Revelation 19:20, 20:10). So it seems that the followers of the Antichrist and the False Prophet may face the same destiny as these two evil individuals do.

Therefore, Bible prophecy experts argue that there will be something extremely serious about the Mark of the Beast that will make those who take it worthy of experiencing such severe divine judgment.

Because of this, it can be inferred that taking the Mark of the Beast will not only mean opting into a particular economic system or method of financial payment during the Tribulation. Taking the Mark must be something that deserves God's unrelenting wrath and judgment, and so it must be a sin.

Furthermore, because of the severity of the punishment that God will inflict on those who take the Mark of the Beast, no one will accidentally or unthinkingly accept the Mark without knowing what it implies.

The Bible clearly says that an angelic messenger will fly around the world to warn everyone what taking the Mark of the Beast will mean for their eternal destinies (Revelation 14:9–11).

There will be no excuse and no possible way for the people who will take the Mark to plausibly complain to God that their judgment is unfair or unjust. They will not be able to claim that they did not know what they were doing when they chose to worship the Antichrist, either by taking the Mark, or worshipping his Image.

The severe punishment is also why it is safe to say that God will not allow the False Prophet or Antichrist to force the Mark on anyone without his or her personal consent. Instead, anyone who refuses and happens to be caught by the authority figures without the Mark will simply be beheaded (Revelation 20:4).

Because of this, children and infants will likely not be permitted to receive the Mark of the Beast. Based on Jesus's love for children (e.g., Matthew 19:13–14), most Christians would say that God would not condemn a child or infant to eternal punishment for something that a parent chose for them. Furthermore, in the Old Testament, God says that children will not be punished for their parents' sins (Ezekiel 18:20).

Although, if sinful habits are passed down from one generation to the next, then subsequent generations will face the same divine punishment as their parents did, but because of their own sins (Exodus 20:5). Yet that situation will not occur during the Tribulation, because each person will have to make his or her own choice to receive or not receive the Mark of the Beast.

Therefore, the Mark of the Beast is not a credit card, a social security number, a driver's license, or anything that people today can sign up for without consciously making a choice to worship the Antichrist as God, or without pledging eternal loyalty and allegiance to the Antichrist.

There may even be a digital currency or personal digital identification that will be implemented at some point during the Tribulation, or maybe even before the Rapture.

However, using digital currency or a digital ID will not be the Mark of the Beast, unless the system also comes with the other features outlined at the start of this chapter, such as requiring a mark in/on the hand or forehead, being associated with the number 666, and giving personal worship and allegiance to the Antichrist rather than God.

Why Will the Punishment For Taking the Mark of the Beast Be So Severe?

Will the sin of worshipping the Antichrist be the only reason that God will severely punish the people who take the Mark of the Beast?

It is true that for anyone to worship anything or anyone other than God is a violation of the first commandment that God gave to the Israelite people (Exodus 20:3, 34:14, Deuteronomy 11:26–28). So, anyone who worships the Antichrist or the Image of the Beast will be sinning.

In the past, God judged people who worshipped idols or promoted idolatry as being worthy of physical death (e.g., Exodus 32, Deuteronomy 13:5-15). Ultimately, everyone who refuses to believe in Jesus as their Savior will also face the second death, which will be eternal (John 3:16-18, Revelation 20:14-15).

So it could be that taking the Mark of the Beast will effectively be an act of blatant and intentional idolatry.

However, although idolatry is a sin, it is unclear why this particular act of blatant idolatry will instantly condemn anyone who worships the Antichrist to such severe and possibly eternal punishment.

Many people throughout history have committed idolatry, but later repented and became true believers in Jesus (1 Corinthians 12:2-3, Acts 17:29-34). Greed is also a form of idolatry (Ephesians 5:5), and Christians are warned that no one can serve both God and money at the same time (Luke 16:13).

Yet putting God as the first priority above all other things (and especially above money), is something that every Christian struggles with in one way or another. Every sin is a choice to reject God's perfect ways, and every Christian will still be a sinner until they die or are raptured (1 John 1:10, 3:2).

The decision about whether to take the Mark of the Beast will be the ultimate choice between God and money that the people who will live during the Tribulation will have to face.

However, ever since Jesus died on the cross, there are no sins that are unforgivable, except the sin of blaspheming the Holy Spirit (Mark 3:28–29). This unforgivable sin was committed by the religious leaders of Jesus' time when they attributed Jesus' miracles and the work of the Holy Spirit to Satan (Matthew 12:22–30).

By saying this, these people resisted the work of the Holy Spirit in their hearts (Acts 7:51), and refused to believe in Jesus as their Messiah. Therefore, their sins were unforgivable, because there is no one else who can forgive sin and provide eternal salvation except for Jesus Christ (Acts 4:12).

But all sin, including idolatry, can be forgiven by repenting and trusting in Jesus as one's personal Savior. Therefore, there must be some aspect of the Mark of the Beast that will be worse than simply prioritizing money instead of God, and far worse than even committing blatant idolatry.

This sin must be something so severe that once someone takes the Mark of the Beast, there will be no longer any possibility of repenting or asking for God's forgiveness.

There is some speculation among prophecy experts that the reason everyone who takes the Mark of the Beast will be condemned to suffer God's torment in the Lake of Fire, along with the Antichrist, the False Prophet, Satan, and all of Satan's angels (Revelation 20:10, Matthew 25:41), is because there is something about the Mark of the Beast that makes those who take the Mark become unable to repent of their sins.

There are two main ways that prophecy experts suggest the Mark of the Beast may make it impossible for people to repent from their sins and be forgiven by God.

Possibility 1: The Mark May Involve Artificial Intelligence and Mind Control

Some prophecy experts speculate that the Mark of the Beast will be some sort of technology that merges people with artificial intelligence. Some technology experts suggest that such a merging will become necessary once artificial intelligence reaches a point where it makes humanity obsolete.

If this is the technology that will be used, then perhaps once the Mark of the Beast is taken, people's minds will become fully controlled by the Antichrist, or by some artificial intelligence that the Antichrist will create.

If so, these people would be unable to ask for forgiveness, because the system controlling their minds would never allow them to think of the possibility.

Prophecy experts who suggest this possibility refer to the Old Testament Book of Daniel. Here, it says that the Antichrist's empire will be more terrible than several other tyrannical empires that came before it (i.e., Babylon, Medo-Persia, and Greece). The Antichrist's empire is also metaphorically described as having large iron teeth, and it will trample down the whole world (Daniel 7:7).

All of these other empires that ruled over Israel were described by Daniel using symbols that involve animals. But suddenly, this last empire that Daniel sees conquering the whole world is described as having a metallic component. So it is suggested that the iron teeth perhaps represent computer technology, and this is what will make this last empire so terrifying and powerful.

That the Antichrist will use digital technology to control the world is consistent with the other details noted earlier, such as how the Mark of the Beast seems to require a digital currency, or at least an exclusive system to perform electronic financial transactions.

The Image of the Beast that will be able to speak might also make use of some sort of advanced artificial intelligence and robotics technology (Revelation 13:15).

So there is a good argument to be made that the Antichrist's kingdom will be a highly technological one— perhaps even a *technocracy*, which would make it different in kind from other past empires and kingdoms, just like Daniel prophesied.

Whether the Mark of the Beast will involve technological mind control of all who opt in to take it, though, is still uncertain.

However, the Bible is clear that those people who are alive during the Tribulation will clearly know what the Mark of the Beast is, and they will know that they must avoid taking it in order to avoid severe divine retribution (Revelation 14:9–11).

Possibility 2: The Mark of the Beast May Change People's Genetic Codes

Another speculative possibility argues that those people who take the Mark of the Beast will not just become unable to repent, but they will actually become *unredeemable.* If so, then even if God wanted to forgive these people and save them, he would be unable to.

This possibility relies on the argument that in order to be redeemable, people must be fully human. This is because Jesus was fully human, and so his death was able to save all those who are genetically descended from Adam and Eve, just like he was (Romans 5:12–19, Hebrews 2:9–17).

Fallen angels are therefore unredeemable, and so the only eternal destiny that is available for Satan and his demons is eternity in the Lake of Fire (Hebrews 2:16, Matthew 25:41).

These facts suggest that if there were some way for the Antichrist to make people become no longer fully human, then Jesus' death would no longer apply to them. They would become just as unredeemable as Satan and his fallen angels are.

Prophecy experts who argue for this possibility suspect that taking the Mark of the Beast will require people to undergo some sort of gene-altering medical treatment, in order for them to receive permission to buy and sell in the Antichrist's digital financial system.

According to this theory, if something were able to rewrite or replace portions of people's DNA with an artificial genetic code, then these people would no longer be fully human, and so they would no longer qualify for salvation by putting their faith in Jesus Christ.

However, if this is what will happen, then the genetic change that will be caused by the Mark of the Beast would have to be something significantly different from the simple copying errors that creep into human DNA naturally during reproduction, which can cause people to suffer from various genetic disorders.

The change caused by the Mark of the Beast would also have to be different from the random DNA damage that can be caused by exposing people's cells to radiation of various kinds.

These sorts of DNA faults are never mentioned in Scripture as making anyone unredeemable, because they are simply an unfortunate side effect of humanity living in an imperfect world, due to the first sin of Adam and Eve.

Admittedly, this interpretation of the Mark of the Beast is speculative, because it is not clear at what point someone's DNA goes from being human to no-longer human. But perhaps it explains why taking the Mark of the Beast is such a terrible thing that it will instantly make anyone who takes it become worthy of suffering eternal divine torment in the Lake of Fire.

Yet some support for this interpretation may come from how Jesus mentioned that the end times will be like the days of Noah (Matthew 24:37, Luke 17:26).

Bible interpreters often say that Noah and his family were the very last righteous people who were alive on Earth before the worldwide Flood, while everyone else was continually thinking about doing evil (Genesis 6:5–9). If so, it would be consistent with how Jesus also compared the end times to when the righteous man Lot and his family were living among the wicked inhabitants of Sodom and Gomorrah (Luke 17:28–29, Genesis 19).

However, some prophecy experts argue that there was also a very strange phenomenon in the days of Noah that was corrupting humanity's genes. The evidence for this argument comes from the Nephilim (in Hebrew, *nephilim* means "fallen ones"), who are described in the Bible as being on the Earth before the worldwide Flood (Genesis 6:4).

The word *Nephilim* is sometimes translated as "giants" or "mighty men" in English Bibles. These Nephilim are described as being created when the "sons of God" married and procreated with the "daughters of men" (Genesis 6:1–5).

There is a debate about who the "sons of God" were. Some say this phrase simply means men who were descended from the righteous line of Seth, who was Adam and Eve's third son. In this case, the "daughters of men" are interpreted as being the sinful, immoral, idolatrous daughters of Cain, who was Adam and Eve's first son that became the first murderer.

But it does not make sense why God would have to flood the whole world and destroy everyone except for eight people simply because of regular human intermarriage and sin.

Historically, the Israelites struggled many times when their men married women from other non-Israelite tribes who practiced idolatry, because the women would then lead the men and children into idolatry and immoral activities. The Israelites were judged by God when this happened, but it never required God to destroy everyone because of it.

So some prophecy experts believe that the Nephilim were hybrids between angels and humans, although it is not clear how this is biologically possible. Although it seems very strange to think about, this would be the more consistent interpretation, because the term "sons of God" is also used elsewhere in the Old Testament to refer to angelic beings (Job 1:6).

If this interpretation is correct, then when the Bible says that Noah was "perfect," "upright," or "blameless," in his "generations" (Genesis 6:9), it might not only mean that he and his family were the last righteous people on the planet.

The Hebrew word *tamim*, often translated in Genesis 6:9 into English as words such as "perfect," or "upright," can also mean "complete," or "intact." If the word *tamim* is taken in this sense, then perhaps Noah, his wife, his sons, and his sons' wives were the last people left on Earth who had fully complete, perfect, or "intact" human DNA.

Although it does seem like something almost out of a science fiction novel, this scenario explains why God had to save Noah and his family but destroy the rest of genetically-corrupted humanity.

Because Jesus had to be genetically related to Adam and Eve in order to redeem all of humanity, then God had to preserve humanity's genes from corruption until the time when the Messiah would be born. Otherwise, it would invalidate God's prophecy in Genesis 3:15 that the Messiah would come from the "seed of the woman" (Eve, and later, Mary), and humanity would have been unable to be saved.

Satan would have won by destroying humanity, who are made in the image of God (Genesis 1:26), and replacing them with a species made in the Antichrist's own image. God would have to condemn everyone to the Lake of Fire, just like he will do for Satan (Revelation 20:10).

If this interpretation is true, even if it seems almost unbelievable to some Christians today, then perhaps the Mark of the Beast could function similarly to the mixing of angels and humans that created the Nephilim in Noah's time, by changing people so they will be no longer fully human.

It does seem possible that during the Tribulation, through the Antichrist's and False Prophet's near-miraculous deceptions, plus the threat of being locked out from accessing a digital world economy, most people could be convinced to take some sort of medical treatment that will alter their DNA.

The Antichrist and False Prophet might even portray this genetic alteration as a good thing. Perhaps it will be advertised as an "upgrade" to humanity, or the next step in humanity's evolution, such as is proposed by advocates of transhumanism.

Maybe the Antichrist and False Prophet will even claim that taking the Mark of the Beast will make people become like gods or give them immortality. This is how Satan first lied to Eve in the Garden of Eden, and convinced her to eat the forbidden fruit (Genesis 3:4–5).

So, if the Mark of the Beast will change these people's DNA so that they are no longer fully human, then the world would indeed be once again like the days of Noah. It would also explain why those who take the Mark of the Beast will be condemned to eternal torment in the Lake of Fire, with no chance of being forgiven or redeemed.

A hint that perhaps some sort of medical treatment will be part of the Mark of the Beast is suggested by two Bible passages.

First, at some point during the Tribulation, those people who take the Mark of the Beast will have painful sores appear on their bodies (Revelation 16:2). This reminds some prophecy experts about how some people can have negative reactions to even common medical treatments or medications.

Secondly, part of God's judgment on "Babylon" will be because its merchants were very notable and powerful people who deceived the whole world through "sorcery" (Revelation 18:23). In Greek, the word for "sorcery" is *pharmakeia*. English words like *pharmacy* and *pharmaceutical* can be traced back to this same Greek word. So it is suggested that perhaps the Mark of the Beast will have some sort of deceptive pharmaceutical component which will change people's genes.

Yet prophecy experts who propose this interpretation do not usually intend to demonize all medicine or doctors. The Apostle Luke, for example, was a doctor. Some medical treatments and medicines are also mentioned in Scripture as being good things (e.g., 1 Timothy 5:23, Proverbs 17:22, Jeremiah 30:13, Ezekiel 47:12, Revelation 3:18).

Whatever the Mark of the Beast will actually be, the effect of the Antichrist's Mark on those who take is it certain. The moment anyone takes the Mark, they are guaranteed to experience the terrible divine punishment that the Bible warns about.

SUMMARY ABOUT THE MARK OF THE BEAST

Ultimately, all of these details about exactly what the Mark of the Beast may involve are speculation at this point, even if there are some Bible verses that possibly support such interpretations. Perhaps the Mark will actually be something that no one can currently imagine.

Therefore, all that truly matters is that during the Tribulation, the Mark of the Beast will be a very important thing to avoid taking. This is true even if rejecting the Mark will make it difficult to survive without the ability to buy and sell, and even if rejecting the Mark will ultimately cost some individuals their lives.

It will also be very clear what the Mark of the Beast is to the people who are on Earth at that time. It will be identifiable by how it will meet all of the criteria listed at the start of this chapter.

No one will be able to take it accidentally or unknowingly, because an angel will ensure that everyone knows exactly what they are opting into, and will warn them about the terrible punishment that will be the result if they do so.

Therefore, if you are reading this book during the Tribulation, do *not* take the Mark of the Beast! Also make sure to warn others to avoid taking the Mark of the Beast at all costs.

Will Christians Be Able To Take the Mark of the Beast?

Some good news, however, is that all the people who will believe in Jesus Christ after the Rapture can be confident that they will *not* take the Mark of the Beast, regardless of what consequences they will face for rejecting the Mark.

This is because once a person believes in Jesus, his or her eternal inheritance in Heaven is guaranteed, due to the sealing of the Holy Spirit (Ephesians 1:13–14, 4:30, Philippians 1:6).

Therefore, anyone who truly believes in Jesus as his or her Savior will not be able to take the Mark of the Beast, or it would lead to a paradox for their eternal destiny. Someone cannot be sealed by the Holy Spirit to guarantee their eternal future in heaven, and also be condemned to an eternity in the Lake of Fire.

So it is clear that the Holy Spirit will give those faithful saints who are alive on Earth during the Tribulation the strength to refuse taking the Mark of the Beast, even if it means they may be executed for this refusal. Yet any saints who will die for refusing the Mark will be rewarded by being resurrected to rule with Jesus during his Millennial Kingdom (Revelation 20:4).

For those saints and other people who will refuse the Mark of the Beast and manage to avoid being executed, they will only have to survive for another forty-two months until Jesus will destroy the Antichrist and his totalitarian government, including the Mark of the Beast system (Revelation 13:5).

Jesus' return to Earth will be examined in more detail in the next chapter.

Chapter 8

The Purpose of the Tribulation and the Second Coming of Jesus

What is the purpose of the Tribulation?

Why will God send all these awful divine judgments on the world? Isn't God all-good, all-powerful, and all-loving?

Why will God allow the Antichrist to gain power over the whole world and persecute the saints (Revelation 13:5–8)? Why will God allow the False Prophet to force everyone to take the Mark of the Beast, or else they will be persecuted and possibly killed (Revelation 13:11–18)?

There are actually several different reasons why a good and loving God would act in this manner. Ultimately, God has several good goals that he will achieve during the Tribulation period.

After all, God *is* love (1 John 4:8). God is also perfect light and the source of all life, and there is no darkness or evil in him at all (John 1:3–5, 1 John 1:5). God is the creator of every good and perfect gift (James 1:17). God does not want anyone to experience eternal death, but for everyone to repent and be saved (1 Timothy 2:3–4, 2 Peter 3:9, Ezekiel 18:23).

Therefore, God does not cause the Tribulation simply because he is mean, hateful, unfair, or unjust. He does not want to destroy the world out of spite, like how a spoiled child might destroy a toy when the child does not get his or her way.

Instead, God has very good purposes in mind that the Tribulation is necessary to fulfill. It will be yet another example of God bringing good out of something that Satan and sinful humans intended for evil (e.g., Genesis 50:20).

God has promised that everything ultimately works together for the good of those people who love God (Romans 8:28). This includes even something as awful as the Tribulation.

God has specific purposes that will be achieved during the Tribulation for three main groups of people. Each of these purposes will be completed at or shortly after Jesus' Second Coming.

The first group includes people who are descended from the twelve tribes of Israel, and who did not have faith in Jesus before the Rapture.

During the Tribulation, two-thirds of this group of people will be killed, but at the end, the remaining one-third will finally believe that Jesus is their promised Messiah (Zechariah 12:10–14, 13:8–9). These survivors will see the establishment of Jesus's Millennial Kingdom, which will be the fulfillment of all of God's promises that were made to Israel in the Old Testament.

The second group includes all the other people who are not descended from the twelve tribes of Israel, and who also did not have faith in Jesus before the Rapture.

After the Rapture, some of these people will believe in Jesus and so will have eternal life, but others will not believe. The Tribulation will be the ultimate test that will reveal what is in the hearts of everyone who was left behind. During the Tribulation, everyone will have to make a clear choice either for or against Jesus, and this choice will seal their eternal destinies (Matthew 13:24–30).

At the end of the Tribulation, God will remove any surviving unbelievers from the world at the Sheep and Goats Judgment, so that Jesus' Millennial Kingdom will begin with only true believers who will desire to obey him (Matthew 25:31–46).

True believers in Jesus who survive the Tribulation will enter the Millennial Kingdom in their natural mortal bodies. They will have the promise of receiving eternal life, just like anyone else who has believed in Jesus and God throughout all of history. But these people will also be able to marry and repopulate the world, and they will instruct their children in God's ways (Psalm 22:27–31).

The third group of people that God has purposes for includes all the evil people and world leaders who will side with Satan and the Antichrist during the Tribulation. They will have cooperated with Satan's plans to deceive the world and exterminate the saints who will believe in Jesus after the Rapture.

During the Tribulation, God will punish these people for their sins, and ultimately destroy them (Revelation 11:18, 18:23–24). At Jesus' second coming, all of the world's governments and systems that opposed Jesus will also be destroyed (Daniel 2:44–45).

All three of these purposes will be completed by the end of the Tribulation, or just after Jesus' Second Coming. These purposes will be explored in more detail in the rest of this chapter.

Preparing Israel and the World For Jesus' Millennial Kingdom

Throughout this book, it has been mentioned that the Tribulation will last for approximately seven years, or 2520 days, to be exact.

The reason it will be seven years can be traced to a prophecy in the Book of Daniel. The angel Gabriel informed Daniel of a timeline relating to God's purposes for Israel. This timeline involved seventy "weeks" (seventy periods of seven years) which God allotted to Israel and its capital city of Jerusalem in order to achieve several of God's purposes (Daniel 9:24).

The purposes listed in this verse are somewhat cryptic, but they become clear once they are filled out with more information found elsewhere in the Bible. Listed in the chronological order in which they will be fulfilled, these purposes include:

1. For the Messiah to come to Israel and atone for sin, thus defeating both death and the devil.

This was fulfilled in 33 AD when Jesus died on the cross for all of humanity's sins (1 John 2:2, Hebrews 10:11–13). Jesus was the offspring of Abraham who God said would be a blessing to the whole world (Acts 3:25–26, Galatians 3:16).

Jesus was also the promised "seed of the woman" (i.e., Eve, and the virgin Mary). Through Jesus' temporary suffering and death, he succeeded in defeating the "serpent" (i.e., Satan). Jesus will finally destroy Satan completely at the end of Jesus' Millennial Kingdom (Genesis 3:15, Revelation 20:7–10).

2. For Israel to recognize Jesus as their anointed Messiah, and the rightful king of Israel, who will inherit David's throne forever (Isaiah 9:6–7, Luke 1:31–32, Acts 2:22–36).

This will occur at the end of the Tribulation, when the remaining one-third of Jews will call out for their Messiah to save them from the Antichrist's armies (Zechariah 13:8–9, Matthew 23:39).

When they see Jesus returning from Heaven to save them, and that he is crowned as the King of Kings and Lord of Lords (Revelation 19:11–16), then they will be sorry for their people's two-thousand-year rejection of him. This realization will cause them to mourn like someone who has lost their only child (Zechariah 12:10–14).

3. To end Israel's tendency to rebel against God (Ezekiel 39:7–8, 39:21–29).

This prophecy will be fulfilled during Jesus' Millennial Kingdom, when Jesus will rule the world from Jerusalem with a metaphorical rod of iron. Then, under his perfect government, the world will be full of righteousness and peace (e.g., Isaiah 9:6–7, 11:1–10, Zechariah 14:16–21, Micah 4:1–8).

4. To fulfill all Bible prophecy. There will come a time when no more prophecies will be necessary, be-

cause everything will have been fulfilled (1 Corinthians 13:8).

All Bible prophecy will be fulfilled by the end of Jesus' Millennial Kingdom, after the final rebellion of unbelievers takes place. Then Satan will be thrown into the Lake of Fire, death and hell will no longer exist, and everyone whose name is written in the Book of Life will have eternal life (Revelation 20:7–15).

God will finally be "all in all," because all that will be left is the eternal New Heavens and New Earth, where there will no longer be any sin, suffering, or death (Revelation 21:1–8, 1 Corinthians 15:28).

Large parts of Daniel's prophecy relate to the people of Israel. This is because Israel, as the descendants of Abraham, Isaac, and Jacob (who was renamed Israel), were chosen by God in order for them to be a blessing to the rest of the world (Genesis 12:1–3, Exodus 19:5–6, Acts 13:46–47).

The Israelites were given God's law by Moses who went up Mount Sinai to be in God's presence (Exodus 20:1–21). The law was meant to be a good thing, because if it had been followed, it would have brought Israel many blessings (Deuteronomy 28:1–14).

The law also foreshadowed what Jesus would do, and acted as a tutor for God's people until the Messiah would come and fulfill the law (Galatians 3:15–29, Matthew 5:17, Hebrews 8:1–13, 10:1–10).

Yet throughout history, despite how God miraculously rescued the Israelites from Egypt, performed miracles to provide for the Israelites' needs for forty years in the wilderness, and gave Israel the blessing of the law, ancient Israel had difficulty remaining faithful to God (Isaiah 65:1–7).

God judged Israel in various ways for their repeated rejection of him. Often, this involved allowing Israel's enemies to conquer and oppress the people. The people would often repent and cry out to God to save them, and then God would raise up a leader to defeat their enemies. Yet soon the people would again ignore and reject God. This pattern repeated again and again, as shown in the Book of Judges.

Eventually, even Israel's kings and priests ignored God's law, and instead promoted idolatry and immorality. God sent many warnings to his people through his prophets to try to convince them to repent, but they did not.

Therefore, God allowed northern Israel to be conquered by the Assyrians. Soon after, the Babylonians were allowed to conquer southern Israel. Many Israelites were killed in these invasions, while the rest were deported from the land of Israel (Jeremiah 25:1–12, Ezekiel 12:8–16).

As Jeremiah had prophesied, the Jews were exiled from their land for exactly seventy years (Jeremiah

25:11, Daniel 9:1–2). This is why the prophet Daniel was living in Babylon (Daniel 1:1–7).

Daniel was a faithful believer in God, and he regretted the sins that his people had committed before their exile. Through prayer, he asked God to forgive them and to have mercy on his people once again (Daniel 9:3–19). In response to this prayer, God sent the angel Gabriel to deliver the prophecy of the seventy "weeks" (sometimes translated as "sevens") to Daniel, to comfort him by giving him an outline of God's plans for Israel's future.

Most Bible commentators agree that the term "week" or "seven" used in Daniel 9:24–27 means seven years. So altogether, this prophecy deals with a period of time that adds up to 490 years. However, there is some confusion over exactly when these seventy "weeks" of Daniel's prophecy began.

It is often thought that the seventy "weeks" began when Persian King Cyrus allowed the Jews to return to Israel and rebuild the Temple, after they had been exiled for seventy years. This occurred in 538 BC (Ezra 1:1–4), exactly as had been prophesied (Isaiah 44:24–28, Jeremiah 25:11).

However, Daniel's prophecy said that the true starting point of the seventy "weeks" began from the command to rebuild the city of Jerusalem itself (Daniel 9:25). This happened in 444 BC, when King Artaxerxes gave Nehemiah permission to return to Israel and begin organizing the people and obtaining the supplies to reconstruct Jerusalem (Nehemiah 2:1–8).

Using the date given in Nehemiah 2:1, prophecy experts have calculated the end date for the first sixty-nine "weeks" or 483 years of Daniel's prophecy.

To do the calculation correctly, one must use 360 days for each of the 483 years, as was used at the time in both Babylonian and Hebrew calendars. Then it must be remembered that only one year passes between 1 BC and 1 AD. The calculation must also adjust for leap years in the Western calendar. If this calculation is done correctly, it reveals that the sixty-ninth "week" ended in 33 AD, near the end of March.

Thus, the first sixty-nine weeks of Daniel's prophecy ended the same week that Jesus entered Jerusalem on a donkey, which was a way of proclaiming himself to be Israel's long-awaited king (Zechariah 9:9, Luke 19:28–40).

However, Israel's religious leaders rebelled against God yet again when they rejected Jesus as their Messiah, turned the people against him, and arranged for him to be crucified by the Romans (e.g., John 11:45–57, 18:1–40, 19:1–16).

The crucifixion of Jesus ended Daniel's sixty-ninth week, and fulfilled how Daniel prophesied that the "Anointed One" (a.k.a., the Messiah/Christ) would be "cut off," and appear to have achieved nothing

(Daniel 9:26). The term "cut off" is a euphemism for being killed (e.g., Genesis 9:11, Exodus 9:15, Joshua 11:21).

As a result of how Israel rejected and killed their Messiah, God allowed most of Israel from that time onward to be spiritually blinded to the fact that Jesus truly is their Messiah (Romans 11:1-11).

So after Jesus' death, the period of sixty-nine "weeks" was finished, with only one "week" (seven years) remaining in Daniel's prophecy. This final "week" will only begin once the Antichrist signs the peace covenant between Israel and "many" (Daniel 9:27).

During the long gap of time between the sixty-ninth and seventieth "weeks" of years, God shifted his focus from Israel to taking the gospel message to the rest of the world through the Apostle—especially the Apostle Paul (Matthew 28:16-20, Acts 13:44-49, Romans 11:11-24).

Everyone who would believe in Jesus during the time from Jesus' resurrection until the Rapture are part of the Church, including the small number of Jews who have believed that Jesus is their Messiah. In the Church, faith in Jesus makes everyone equal, even Jews and Gentiles (Galatians 3:28, 1 Corinthians 12:13).

God's plan to create the Church was a mystery that was not revealed to the Old Testament prophets (Ephesians 3:1–12). This is why the gap between the sixty-ninth and seventieth "weeks" in Daniel's prophecy seems unexpected.

However, Paul hinted that at some point in the future, God will once again return his focus to Israel. God will bring them back to faith in Jesus after the mostly-Gentile Church has been removed in the Rapture (Romans 11:17–32).

During the Tribulation, Israel will realize how evil the Antichrist is once he desecrates their rebuilt Temple by declaring himself to be God in it (2 Thessalonians 2:3–4).

Jesus told those who are in Judea that when the Antichrist enters the Holy of Holies, they should immediately escape to the mountains for the rest of the Tribulation period (Matthew 24:15–21). This would make sense if the Antichrist will turn on Israel and attempt to kill many of the Jews living in Judea just after his desecration of the Temple (Revelation 12:13–15).

The Antichrist's hatred of the Jews should not be surprising, given Satan's hatred of Israel. Satan has always hated Israel, thanks to how God chose them to be the people from whom the Messiah would come, and who God used to communicate his word to the world, via the inspired human authors who wrote the Old Testament. All of the inspired human authors of the New Testament were also Jews.

Satan has always been at war with God by trying to ruin God's plan of salvation. To do this, Satan has two main targets: Israel, and Israel's Messiah. In Revelation chapter 12, Jesus is described as being the promised Messianic child of Israel who will rule the world with his rod of iron during his Millennial Kingdom (Revelation 12:1–5, 19:15, Psalm 2:8–9).

To try to ruin this prophecy, Satan attempted to kill Jesus several times during his First Coming, before Jesus' mission was complete. Yet Satan failed repeatedly (Matthew 2:16–18, Luke 4:29–30, John 8:58–59, 10:31–39), until the time came for Jesus to be crucified. Then, Jesus allowed himself to be arrested and killed, to fulfill God's plan to save humanity from sin (Matthew 26:36–56, Luke 22:39–53). Forty days after his resurrection, Jesus ascended to Heaven, placing him beyond Satan's reach (Acts 1:6–11, Revelation 12:5).

However, Satan has not given up on ruining God's plans for humanity. At some point during the Tribulation, a spiritual war will break out in Heaven. Satan and his demons will be defeated by Michael and his angels, causing Satan to be thrown down to the Earth. When this occurs, Satan will know that he only has a short time left, and so his next attempt to ruin God's plan will be to try to destroy Israel (Revelation 12:7–12, Daniel 12:1).

Satan will try to destroy all of the Jews because if there were no Jews left alive, then none of them would be able to call out for Jesus to return, which is a precondition of Jesus' Second Coming (Matthew 23:38–39).

If he were successful in this goal, Satan could theoretically prevent Jesus' Second Coming. Doing so would mean that this prophecy could not be fulfilled, thus making God a liar, and showing that Satan is more powerful than God. Satan knows that it is prophesied that his plans will fail, but this will not stop him from trying.

Thus, once Satan loses the heavenly war and is thrown down to Earth, and the Antichrist declares himself to be God in the rebuilt Temple, Jesus' instructions for everyone who is in Judea to immediately flee is quite understandable (Matthew 24:16–21).

God will help these people escape from the Antichrist's pursuit, and they will find shelter and supernatural protection in a hiding place (Revelation 12:13–16). This hiding place is often thought to be the ancient ruins of Selah or Petra, in Jordan, close to Bozrah. This line of thinking comes from a prophecy that seems to describe these people being the first ones to be rescued from destruction at Jesus' Second Coming (Isaiah 63:1–6).

So at the end of the Tribulation, after the remaining one-third of Jews have called out to their Messiah, Jesus will finally return by appearing in the clouds for his Second Coming (Matthew 26:63–64, Acts 1:9–11).

He will be riding a white horse, and wearing a robe dipped in his own blood that symbolizes his crucifixion, with many crowns on his head that show he is truly the King of Kings and Lord of Lords. The armies of Heaven will follow behind him on white horses (Revelation 19:11–16, Jude 14–15). These heavenly angelic armies are usually invisible, but are sometimes visible if God permits (2 Kings 6:15–17).

Even in the Old Testament, the Son of God was seen as the commander of God's armies. He was sometimes referred to as the Angel of the Lord in the few instances when he appeared on Earth before he became incarnate as the human named Jesus (e.g., Joshua 5:13–15, Judges 2:1–4, 2 Kings 19:35).

This does not mean that the Son of God was an angel, in the sense of being a non-divine created spiritual entity, because in Scripture the term *angel* can also simply mean a "messenger."

The Son of God has always been equal with God the Father, because they are both part of the same Triune being of God, along with the Holy Spirit (e.g., John 10:30). This is why the Angel of the Lord accepts people's worship (Joshua 5:14–15), but other angels refuse to be worshipped, because only God should be worshipped (Revelation 19:10).

Jesus' return at his Second Coming will be like lightning that flashes across the entire sky, and every person on Earth will somehow see him (Matthew 24:27, Revelation 1:7).

His army will include the two-thirds of all angels who remained faithful to God (Revelation 12:4). It will also include all the raptured and resurrected Christians who will return with Jesus from Heaven, where they had been for the last seven years of the Tribulation (John 14:1–3, Isaiah 26:20–21).

It is certain that these Christians will be accompanying Jesus at his Second Coming, because after the Rapture, the Church will always be wherever Jesus is (1 Thessalonians 4:17). Christians will also need to be on Earth in order to serve in their roles in Jesus' perfect government during the Millennial Kingdom (Luke 19:11–19).

Yet it is unclear whether these heavenly armies will actually fight in the Battle of Armageddon. It seems that it will be primarily Jesus' divine word, represented by the sword that John depicted as coming from Jesus' mouth, that kills most of the human opposition (Revelation 19:15). This is appropriate, because it was also God's Word (a.k.a. the eternal Son of God) who spoke creation into existence (John 1:1–3, Hebrews 11:3).

In contrast, an anonymous angel will be assigned to capture Satan and throw him into the bottomless pit, where he will be locked up for a thousand years (Revelation 20:1–3). This shows that Satan is no match for Jesus, or even for other righteous angels.

After rescuing the people at Petra and Bozrah, Jesus will rescue the people who remain alive in Judah and Jerusalem from the armies that the Antichrist will have assembled together at *Har Megiddo* (Revelation 16:13–16, Zechariah 12:7–9).

Obviously, Jesus will win this battle. All the armies that the Antichrist will have assembled against Jerusalem will be destroyed in a terrible way. The soldiers' bodies will rapidly rot away, even while the soldiers are still standing on their feet. The soldiers will also attack each other, and a plague will destroy their supply camps (Zechariah 14:12–15).

Jesus' Second Coming will be complete once he lands on the Mount of Olives in Jerusalem. The moment his foot touches it, there will be an earthquake. The mountain will split in half, and create a valley that survivors in Jerusalem will flee through (Zechariah 14:3–5).

The geography of Israel will be significantly changed as a result of this earthquake. Jerusalem's elevation will increase (Micah 4:1), but other parts of the country will become flat. There will also be changes to the rivers (Zechariah 14:8–11).

The changes in the rivers will help the land of Israel become very fertile, just like God promised it will be during Jesus' Millennial Kingdom (Ezekiel 47:7–12, Isaiah 35:1–7, Amos 9:13–15).

The Destruction of the World's Governments

Once the Battle of Armageddon is over, the entire land of Israel will be covered with dead bodies, which will be eaten by birds. The Antichrist and False Prophet will both be captured, and they will be thrown directly into the Lake of Fire (Revelation 19:17–21).

Satan and his demons will be defeated and thrown into the supernatural jail that is called the "bottomless pit" for a thousand years. This will be so that they can no longer deceive the world or inspire people to sin during Jesus' Millennial Kingdom (Revelation 20:1–3).

Jesus' victory at the Battle of Armageddon will therefore complete another purpose of the Tribulation, which will be for God to destroy all of the world's governments and evil leaders and systems (Daniel 2:44–45, 7:11–28). These will be replaced by Jesus' perfect government (Revelation 11:15).

Jesus' government will include those Christians who died for their faith during the Tribulation. They will be resurrected at some point after the Battle of Armageddon, and they will rule with Jesus for at least a thousand years (Revelation 20:4–6).

The twelve disciples will rule over Israel, as sub--rulers under Jesus (Matthew 19:28, Luke 22:30).

The raptured and resurrected Christians who made up the Church will also make up a large part of Jesus' righteous government, just like they are promised in various places in Scripture (e.g., Revelation 2:26–27, 3:21, 2 Timothy 2:11–13).

Christians will be rewarded for how they used their resources and abilities to serve God during their lives. Their reward will be to have ruling authority over various numbers of cities after Jesus' Second Coming (Luke 19:11–27).

Jesus' Millennial Kingdom will be run perfectly, because all the resurrected and raptured saints will finally have perfect hearts and minds, so they will never sin again (1 John 3:2, Philippians 1:6). There will be no government corruption, bribery, or unjust judges that cause so many problems for the world today.

God's ideal vision of leadership is that the greatest leader should serve everyone, rather than the leaders being served by everyone (Matthew 20:25–28). So whoever were the best servants of Jesus during their earthly lives will be the most highly-regarded rulers in Jesus' kingdom (Mark 9:34–35). Probably, these people will have been quite obscure and unimportant during their earthly lives, because Jesus said that in his kingdom, some of the last will be first, and some of the first will be last (Luke 13:29–30).

Jesus and his perfect government will rule the world strictly, which is represented by the use of a rod of iron (Psalm 2:7–9, Revelation 2:27, 12:5, 19:15). This rod represents Jesus' discipline, which is for people's own good (e.g., Proverbs 13:24, Hebrews 12:5–11).

During his Millennial Kingdom, Jesus will keep sin closely in check, so that it cannot once again spread and ruin the blessed righteousness that the world will experience during that time (Isaiah 9:6–7, 11:1–5, Zechariah 14:16–21, Micah 4:1–8). People who blatantly refuse to obey God will die at a hundred years old, while those who generally obey him will live much longer (Isaiah 65:19–23), perhaps even until the end of the Jesus' Millennial Kingdom.

In this way, during Jesus' Millennial Kingdom, the world will see a return to the long lifespans that people had before the Flood. There, the oldest person ever recorded lived to 969 years old (Genesis 5:27).

After all of the divine judgments during the Tribulation, the world will seem to be in a terrible condition. All of the world's oceans and rivers will have been turned to blood (Revelation 16:3–4), and a third of the trees and all grass will have been burned up (Revelation 8:7).

Yet it appears that after Jesus' Second Coming, he will miraculously restore the planet's environment. There are many wonderful prophecies about this in the Old Testament.

For example, during the Millennial Kingdom, springs of water will appear in deserts and allow the deserts to bloom with vegetation (Isaiah 35:1–7). Many types of fish will flourish, and fruit trees will grow along the banks of freshwater rivers (Ezekiel 47:7–12).

Animals and livestock that need pastures will have more than enough food (Isaiah 30:23–24). Food will grow so easily that human farmers will have difficulty harvesting the enormous amount of crops before it will be time to plant again (Amos 9:13). People will live in houses with their own vineyards and fruit trees (Amos 9:14, Micah 4:4).

Even the animals will be somehow changed to live at peace with one another, because they will all eat plants. Poisonous snakes or other dangerous animals will no longer be a threat, even to human children (Isaiah 11:6–7, 65:25).

In this way, during the Millennial Kingdom, nature will no longer suffer like it did during the thousands of years when it was cursed due to the sin of Adam and Eve (Romans 8:19–23). The planet will enjoy almost Eden-like conditions once again.

The people during this time will love to live in an environment like this, and there will be much prosperity (Jeremiah 31:10–14).

People will be generally obedient to God, and will go up to celebrate the Old Testament feasts in Jerusalem again, although there will also be negative consequences if they do not (Zechariah 14:16–19).

Knowledge of God will be ubiquitous, so there will no longer be any need for people to evangelize or teach each other about God and God's ways (Jeremiah 31:34).

The Judgment of the Nations

Now, this raises the question of who will be ruled by Jesus and his saints during Jesus' Millennial Kingdom.

The people who will survive the Tribulation and go on to repopulate the world during Jesus' Millennial Kingdom will at least include one-third of the people of Israel (Zechariah 13:8–9). They will have recognized Jesus as their Messiah, and will become obedient and faithful to God throughout Jesus' Millennial Kingdom.

However, Jesus will also need to judge the rest of the people around the world, in order to determine who will be permitted to live in the Millennial Kingdom (Matthew 13:24–30, 13:36–43, 13:47–50,

25:31–46). This is the third purpose of the Tribulation, as well as the purpose of the judgment that will occur shortly after Jesus' return, which is known as the Sheep and Goats Judgment.

In summary, anyone who refuses to repent from their sins and believe in Jesus during the Tribulation will not be worthy of entering Jesus' Millennial Kingdom.

Some of these people will experience physical death during the Tribulation, which will occur in many different ways during the twenty-one divine judgments that will occur during those seven years. Their physical deaths will be followed by the second death after the Final Judgment takes place, sometimes after Jesus' Millennial Kingdom (Revelation 20:11–15).

However, because God does not want anyone to experience eternal death, part of the purpose for sending the judgments of the Tribulation will be to try to convince them to wake up, repent from their sins, and put their faith in Jesus Christ so they can have eternal life.

This is the same reason that God said he would send disasters on Israel when they turned away from him (Deuteronomy 28:15–68, 30:1–3). If the people who experience these awful judgments during the Tribulation will repent, then these punishments will simply be an act of God's discipline, which is ultimately done for people's good (Hebrews 12:5–11).

After all, there is no value in keeping one's life safe now, only to lose it eternally because of lack of faith in Jesus Christ (Mark 8:34–38).

Unfortunately, even though the judgments of the Tribulation will be terrible, most people will not repent (Revelation 9:20–21, 16:9–11). Therefore, like in the time before the worldwide Flood, God will once again be required to destroy evil people to keep them from overrunning the world (Genesis 6:5–6, 2 Peter 3:7).

This is how God has operated throughout all of human history. Whenever evil grows too influential, God will send warnings that he plans to judge and destroy those evil people who refuse to repent. However, God always saves and preserves the lives of those who do repent, and he will begin society again with these survivors so that humanity is not completely destroyed (e.g., Psalm 11).

Another instance of when a judgment like this occurred was at the Tower of Babel. There, the people who were descended from Noah were instructed to spread out and repopulate the world after the Flood (Genesis 9:1). But they refused, and instead gathered together to build a tall tower.

There must have been some sort of evil or sinful purpose behind the construction of this tower, because God was displeased with this activity. As a judgment on the people, God he decided to disrupt their language, so that they could not continue building the tower. The people then had to separate into smaller groups who shared a common language, and they spread out around the world as God had intended (Genesis 11:1-9).

Perhaps the need to limit the destructiveness of evil people is also why after the Flood, God chose to gradually reduce the human lifespan down to less than a hundred and twenty years (Genesis 6:3). God also gave Noah permission to institute the death penalty for murderers (Genesis 9:6).

In this way, no individual could inflict evil on the world for nearly as long as they could have done before the Flood, when some people lived for hundreds of years. Also, ideally, anyone who was once proven to be a murderer would be prevented from murdering anyone else.

During the time of the Tower of Babel, God said that if the people were united and able to cooperate fully, then eventually, nothing would be impossible for them to achieve (Genesis 11:6). If evil people became united in this way, they could do significant harm to righteous people and also the planet.

The ultimate proof of how destructive sinful humanity can be will be seen during the Tribulation. Then, once again, all of humanity will be united in a common purpose, but this time, under the leadership of the Antichrist.

As discussed in Chapter 7, if the Mark of the Beast is as terrible as it seems it might be, if God did not end the Tribulation earlier, humanity itself might be corrupted beyond the point of salvation (Revelation 14:9–11). All of the righteous people who rejected the Mark of the Beast would eventually be tracked down and eliminated (Revelation 13:7). Only the evil God-rejecting people would be left alive, and they would all have to be destroyed at Jesus' Second Coming (Matthew 24:22, Mark 13:20).

Thus, at the end of the Tribulation, humanity will have had the ultimate demonstration of just how evil the human heart can be (Genesis 6:5, Jeremiah 17:9). The Tribulation will also prove that God's ways are superior and should be followed because they lead to life and blessings, while sin only leads to suffering and death (Deuteronomy 30:19–20, James 1:15, Romans 6:20–23).

Jesus' Millennial Kingdom will also prove this same point, but in a different way. There, under the strict government of Jesus and his perfected saints, sin will be kept in check, and the world will experience far more righteousness and blessing than it has had since the Garden of Eden.

But even then, the mortal people will still have the same sinful hearts as before. Those who are not outwardly rebellious, and so do not die at a hundred years old, will still likely wish that they could throw away God's rules, just like all sinners do (e.g., Psalm 2:1–3, Romans 7:7–12).

The inwardly rebellious hearts of the mortal people living under Jesus' righteous government are the reason that at the end of the thousand years, Jesus will release Satan from the bottomless pit and allow him to go free for a short time. Satan will deceive people all around the world and convince them that despite how wonderful it has been for them during Jesus' Millennial Kingdom, it is worthwhile to attempt to rebel against God one last time.

Then, much like during the Tribulation, people will have to make a final choice regarding whose side they will be on: God's, or Satan's. Those who side with Satan will surround Jerusalem in an attempt to overthrow Jesus' government, but God will destroy the rebels with fire that comes down from Heaven. Satan will then be finally thrown into the Lake of Fire (Revelation 20:7–10).

This final rebellion will be the ultimate proof that humanity's sin problem is truly caused by the sinful human heart (Genesis 6:5, Jeremiah 17:9). Having lived for a thousand years under a perfect and incorruptible government, while enjoying the beauty and prosperity of divinely-blessed nature, the only excuse for why people would choose to rebel against Jesus will be because they gave in to their sinful nature that was inherited from Adam and Eve (Romans 5:12–19).

Returning to the start of the Tribulation, the good news is that many people will finally believe in Jesus after the Rapture happens, and they see the first few judgments of the Tribulation beginning to occur (Revelation 7:9–17). Sometimes it is only when people's lives are disrupted or they face danger that they begin to realize their need for God.

So those people who turn back to God because they suffered or faced hard times will ultimately be glad that they experienced it, because through their difficulties, God will have saved them. Then in the end, after the final judgment, these people will get to experience the eternal New Heavens and New Earth, where there will be no more suffering ever again, and so their temporary suffering will become infinitely insignificant (Revelation 21:1–4, 2 Corinthians 4:16–18, Romans 8:18).

However, not all of these people who repent during the Tribulation will necessarily make it into the Millennial Kingdom. To have this privilege, they will have to be on the correct side of the Sheep and Goats Judgment.

The Sheep and Goats Judgment

This judgment will occur sometime soon after Jesus' Second Coming, once he is ready to set up his Millennial Kingdom (Matthew 25:31).

From every nation, everyone who has survived the Tribulation will be gathered by angels, and brought to Jerusalem to face Jesus' judgment (Matthew 24:29–31, 25:32–33). He will sort all of these people into one of two categories:

1. Those who were generous and provided for the needs of others during the Tribulation, even if it put themselves at risk.

This action seems to demonstrate some sort of implicit faith in Jesus Christ (Matthew 25:34–40), because these people will be rewarded with eternal life (Matthew 25:46), which is the same reward as is given to all other believers in Jesus. These people will also have refused to take the Mark of the Beast, because the Mark of the Beast dooms everyone who takes it to suffer divine judgment, possibly for all eternity (Revelation 14:9–10).

2. Those who were not generous to others during the Tribulation.

These people will be punished eternally, because this fact shows that they were not true believers in Jesus Christ (Matthew 25:41–46). These people may have taken the Mark of the Beast, but this group might also include other non-Christians who refused the Mark of the Beast and still managed to survive until the end of the Tribulation, but they were not generous toward others.

However, the above two categories do not mention the possibility of there being any true Christians who, because of fear and selfishness, did not act generously toward others during the Tribulation.

Why is this possible group of people not mentioned in Matthew 25:31–46? There are only two plausible answers to this question:

First, the Holy Spirit might be able to influence the hearts of true believers in Jesus Christ during the Tribulation in such a way that not only guarantees that they will refuse the Mark of the Beast, but also guarantees that they will be generous toward others. In this way, all the saints who survive the Tribulation would pass Jesus' judgment and be admitted into his Millennial Kingdom.

However, there is also the possibility that any true believers in Jesus who were not generous during the Tribulation, or who lost their faith at some point during the Tribulation due to persecution, will not physically survive the Tribulation. God may allow these people to be killed in one of the many divine judgments, so that they will not be alive to be judged at the Sheep and Goats judgment.

This second possibility seems to be plausible, based on the parable of the ten virgins as told by Jesus in Matthew 25:1–13.

This parable tells a story of ten young women who are waiting for the bridegroom to return, so that they can go into a wedding celebration. However, the bridegroom arrives late at night, after all the women have fallen asleep.

When the women hear the bridegroom coming, they wake up and try to light their oil lamps. This may refer to a tradition in ancient Israel where at a wedding celebration, young women would do a dance with their lamps as part of the festivities.

However, in the story, only five of the young women are wise and have brought extra oil that they use to re-light their lamps. They do not have enough extra oil to share with the other five women who forgot to bring some. While the five unwise virgins are out trying to find somewhere to buy oil late at night, the bridegroom arrives, and only the wise virgins with lit lamps go into the wedding celebration.

It should be noted that in this story, the bride is not mentioned because she would represent the Church. The bridegroom is not marrying the ten virgins, because polygamy is never endorsed in the Old Testament. (Some famous Old Testament figures did have more than one wife, but this typically led to negative consequences of some sort or another for these families). Thus, the return of the bridegroom represents Jesus' Second Coming, and the wedding celebration represents Jesus' Millennial Kingdom.

Lamps are used to shine a light, and the light itself is Christ (John 8:12). Christians are commanded to let their light (i.e., their faith in Christ) shine through their good works (Matthew 5:15).

During the Tribulation, the saints' faith in Jesus would be shown by being generous to others who also refuse to take the Mark of the Beast, and therefore, have no ability to buy or sell in the Antichrist's economy (Revelation 13:16–18). These faithful saints may also visit fellow saints who were thrown into jail for their faith, and may welcome people into their homes who had to leave their own homes due to disasters or persecution (Matthew 25:35–40).

Some prophecy experts also believe that when Jesus refers to providing generously for "the least of these, my brothers," in Matthew 25:40, he may be also referring specifically to the 144,000 Jewish evangelists who will believe in Jesus during the Tribulation (Revelation 7:1–8, 14:1–5).

These evangelists might operate much like Jesus and the early Apostles did, where they went preaching from town to town, and so depended on people to welcome them into their homes and to provide food for them.

So it could be that the parable of the ten virgins in Matthew 25:1–13 teaches that roughly half of the new believers in Jesus during the Tribulation may quickly lose their faith as a result of the persecutions they will experience. Thus, these saints will not do good works that demonstrate their faith, and so they would not pass the Sheep and Goats Judgment.

It will be impossible for the faithful saints who did good works to transfer any of their faith or good works to these unfaithful saints, just like how the five wise virgins are said to be unable to share their oil with the five unwise virgins. Instead, the five foolish virgins are told to go out and buy oil for themselves, just like how these saints would have to go out and do their own good works.

But it seems there is not enough time, because while the virgins are out trying to buy oil, the bridegroom arrives, and he enters with the five wise virgins into the wedding celebration. The five foolish virgins are locked out of the party.

Similarly, the saints who may lose their faith and therefore not do any good works during the Tribulation will miss out on the joy of experiencing the Millennial Kingdom.

Yet if these saints have truly believed in Jesus, they will have eternal life. This is because the Holy Spirit seals all believers the moment they trust in Jesus as their Savior, and this guarantees that they will have an eternal inheritance in Heaven (Ephesians 1:13–14).

Therefore, it is not true that the saints during the Tribulation are eternally saved on the basis of faith plus good works, while believers in the Church are eternally saved only on the basis of faith, as some prophecy teachers claim.

Everyone who will ever be eternally saved is saved *only* on the basis of God's grace, through faith in Christ alone, and not good works. Otherwise, people could boast and brag that they contributed something to their own salvation (Ephesians 2:8–9). This is why it is only faith that matters, and has ever mattered (Romans 3:23–25).

More information about why faith in Jesus Christ is the only way for anyone to have eternal life is the topic of the next chapter.

Chapter 9

What The End Times Mean For You Today

If you have read all the previous chapters up to this point, then congratulations! You have now been introduced to one of the most complex and least-studied topics within the Bible.

Many Christians go their entire lives without learning as much about the end times as you have read here. Even pastors and theologians are often less informed about the end times than you now are.

Yet none of what you have learned will matter if it does not have any relevance for your life and your relationship with Jesus.

The things talked about in this book relate to only 1,007 years of human history: the seven-year Tribulation, and the thousand-year Millennial Kingdom of Jesus.

However, even such a long period of time is infinitely short in comparison to eternity. Therefore, it is very important for you to know how to make your eternal future secure.

How To Secure Your Eternal Future

The Bible teaches that all people will experience only one of two possible futures:

1. Eternal life in the New Heaven and New Earth.
2. Eternal destruction in the second death, by being thrown into the Lake of Fire (Revelation 20:11–15, 21:7–8, Matthew 7:13–14).

The first option is infinitely more preferable than the second. God truly loves you, and he hopes that you will believe in Jesus as your Savior so that you can have eternal life (John 3:16).

Each and every person, including yourself, was made by God because God loves you and wants to have a personal relationship with you.

God wants you to live in his very own presence on the New Earth, along with Jesus, the holy angels, and all other redeemed people throughout history (Revelation 21:1–4, Hebrews 12:22–24). Your eternal future there will be better than what anyone can currently imagine (1 Corinthians 2:9).

However, there is a problem. All humans who have ever lived are sinners, and therefore, everyone has sinned at least once (Romans 3:23–25, 5:12). So what are sins, and why did Jesus have to die for yours, in order for you to be able to believe in him and have eternal life?

To sin, and to be a sinner, means that you have failed to live a perfectly holy life. Yet God requires his people to be perfectly holy, just like he is (Leviticus 11:45, 1 Peter 1:14–16).

God's perfect holiness means that God always does what is good, right, and loving. There is not even the slightest trace of evil or sin in him (1 John 1:5, James 1:17).

In fact, God *is* perfect love in his innermost being (1 John 4:8). Although there is only one God, God exists as the three equally-divine Persons of the Trinity: God the Father, God the Son, and God the Holy Spirit (e.g., Matthew 3:16–17, 28:19). These three divine Persons have always existed in an eternal relationship of perfect love for one another.

Because God is love, God tells humanity that we would be worthy of eternal life if only we could love God with all our heart, soul, mind, and strength, and also love everyone else just as much as we love ourselves (Luke 10:25–27). Every commandment that God gave to people in the Old Testament can be summarized by these two instructions.

Or, to say the same thing differently, God wants us to do justice, to love kindness, and to always walk in a humble relationship with himself (Micah 6:8).

Unfortunately, no one except for Jesus has ever done that perfectly. Jesus never sinned, although he was tested and tempted in every way (Hebrews 4:15, 1 John 3:5).

Furthermore, because God is perfectly good, holy, loving, and righteous, he *must* judge and destroy sin, because sin is the opposite of God's holiness. If God did not destroy sin, he would not be perfectly good, right, true, or loving. After all, it is sinful to allow evil and sin to go unpunished, because doing so would be acting in an unloving way toward those who are being victimized (e.g., Proverbs 17:15, Leviticus 19:15, Isaiah 5:22–24).

Therefore, God cannot tolerate the existence of sin and evil forever (Habakkuk 1:13). Yet God is patient, loving, and merciful. He can hold back his judgment temporarily, in order to give people time to repent (2 Peter 3:9, Romans 2:4).

Repentance happens when people change their minds about something, such as the change of mind that occurs when people first admit that they are sinners, and believe in Jesus as their Savior. As part of this repentance, people will also realize that their sin is negative and that they should try to stop doing it, although Christians will constantly struggle with sin during their earthly lives (e.g., 1 John 1:8–10, Romans 7:14–25).

But if people do not repent by believing in Jesus, they will face God's punishment for their sins, which is eternal death. Why must sin be punished with eternal death?

God is the creator of everything that exists (Genesis 1:1, Revelation 4:11). God is the ultimate source of all life, love, and light (John 1:1–4). In contrast, all sin inherently leads to death (James 1:15, Romans 6:23). There is no sin that does not hurt someone, somewhere, somehow, and sin also hurts oneself. This is precisely why sin and evil are wrong and unloving, and this is why sin is prohibited by a good and loving God.

Because God is love, anytime we act in a way that is not loving, we are also rejecting God. Therefore, sin always results in the opposite of God: darkness, loneliness, death, and ultimately, eternal destruction in the Lake of Fire, which is the second death (Revelation 20:13–15, Isaiah 66:23–24). The Bible says that anyone who commits even *one* sin is worthy of eternal death (James 2:10)!

When Adam and Eve first sinned by doubting God's word in the Garden of Eden and disobeying his instructions, they became sinners, and so brought misery on themselves and the rest of the world (Genesis 3). The perfect relationship they had with God before then was broken. They were technically worthy of experiencing eternal death that very day, if God had not mercifully postponed his punishment for the length of their mortal lives to give them time to repent (Genesis 2:16–17).

All of Adam and Eve's offspring were also born with a sinful nature, which makes it impossible for them to not sin. Sinning now comes naturally to everyone, and it does not have to be taught to children, who, as soon as they are old enough, begin to show signs of their sinful nature. Because of this sinful nature, and because of our personal sins, everyone is now worthy of experiencing eternal death (Romans 5:12–15).

Despite all this, God still loves everyone. God does not want for anyone to be eternally destroyed, but for everyone to repent and have eternal life (John 3:16, Ezekiel 18:23).

Therefore, God needed a solution that would deal with humanity's sin, while allowing him to justly show mercy to sinful people and forgive individual sinners who repent.

Initially, God taught humanity that sin requires death by allowing people to sacrifice animals as a way to preserve their own lives when they sinned, and to allow sinful people to continue to have a loving relationship with God. These animal sacrifices foreshadowed what God would do later on through Jesus to finally put an end to humanity's sin problem (e.g., Genesis 3:21, 4:4, 8:20, 22:1–14, Job 1:5, Exodus 12:21–32).

This system of sacrifices was further expanded in the instructions that God gave to the descendants of Abraham, Isaac, and Jacob, as is described in much detail in the biblical books of Exodus, Leviticus, and Deuteronomy.

Priests were appointed to perform all these sacrifices and mediate between people and God. There were many complicated rules to follow about how the sacrifices should be performed, and how the priests had to purify themselves in order to even be able to do the sacrifices.

But this system never actually took people's sins away. A better, final sacrifice was necessary to achieve this—one that would be done by a final, perfect High Priest. The sacrifice of the perfect High Priest's own body would take away all sin, once and for all (Hebrews 9:1–28, 10:1–18).

This is why the Son of God, the second Person of the Trinity, came into the world about two thousand years ago as a male human being. This occurred when he was miraculously conceived by the virgin Mary so that he could be born as the baby boy who would be called Jesus (Matthew 1:18–25).

Jesus was the only human who lived a perfect life, and so he was qualified to be humanity's perfect High Priest who did not also need to offer sacrifices for his own sins (Hebrews 7:23–27). This is why Jesus died on the cross for the sins of the world (1 John 2:2, 2 Corinthians 5:19).

Through Jesus' death, he satisfied God's wrath at sin, and eternally saved everyone who would believe in him (Revelation 5:6–9, 2 Corinthians 5:21, Isaiah 53).

Crucifixion was a terrible way to die, and so it was reserved for only the worst criminals. It was so horrible that only the Roman government was allowed to crucify people, and they never did it to their own citizens, unless the individual criminal was a traitor.

Even before he was crucified, Jesus was publicly humiliated, whipped, and beaten almost to the point of death. This is described near the end of each of the biblical books of Matthew, Mark, Luke, and John. Jesus died and was buried, and his body spent three days in a tomb.

But on the third day, Jesus came back to life. He was seen by many eyewitnesses who were completely amazed (e.g., John 20:1–28, 21:1–14, Luke 24:1–43, 1 Corinthians 15:3–7, 2 Peter 1:16).

Jesus's resurrection proved that he truly was the Son of God, and that through his crucifixion, he had defeated the power of death on behalf of everyone who believes in him (Romans 1:3–6, Hebrews 2:14, 1 Corinthians 15:22–25).

And Jesus did all of that for *you*, because he would rather have experienced all of that suffering than for you to miss out on having eternal life with God (Romans 5:7–9).

God's offer of eternal life is completely free for you to accept (Romans 5:15–17, 6:23), and you can do it right now.

All you need to do is to trust that Jesus really is who he said he was—the Son of God—and believe that because of his death on the cross and his bodily resurrection, your sins are now forgiven (John 3:13–18, 3:36, 6:28–29, 1 Corinthians 15:14–17, Romans 4:24–25).

The barrier of sin that had separated you from God is now destroyed, giving you full and complete access to God. You can now have a restored relationship with Jesus, God the Father, and the Holy Spirit, and an amazing eternal future (Mark 15:37–38, Hebrews 10:19–22).

If you have never done so, you can speak to God today through prayer, right where you are. Simply admit that you are a sinner, and ask for God's mercy and grace, on the basis of Jesus' death for your sins. God promises that if you just ask him, he will forgive all your sins (1 John 1:9, Luke 18:9–14, Romans 10:9–13).

If you now believe that Jesus is your Savior, you are guaranteed that you will experience eternity in the New Heavens and New Earth with God (Ephesians 1:13–14).

There is nothing else you need to do. Nothing that you do, such as good works, can ever contribute toward earning your eternal salvation (Ephesians 2:8-9, Romans 3:20, Galatians 2:16). There is also nothing you can do that could make you lose your salvation.

However, you can thank God for all that he has done for you, and thank Jesus for dying for you. You can do this by talking to him either out loud, or silently in your thoughts.

Talking to God like this is called prayer, and you can do it anytime, anywhere. How you pray is not important, because God knows what you want to say even before you finish saying it (Matthew 6:6-8, Psalm 139:4). Draw near to God through prayer, by talking to him about anything you are concerned about, and God will draw close to you and speak to you in your heart through the Holy Spirit (James 4:8, Hebrews 4:16).

Now, if you have believed in Jesus Christ's death and resurrection for your sins, your eternal future is secure. Nothing can separate you from God's love (John 6:37, 10:27-30, Romans 8:31-39).

However, depending on when you have believed in Jesus in regard to when the Rapture happens, you will have a very different experience of the rest of your earthly future in this world. Thus, some final instructions are provided for you in the next two sections.

A Detailed Biblical Introduction To The End Times

IF YOU ARE READING THIS BEFORE THE RAPTURE

If you are fortunate enough to be reading this before the Rapture occurs, then you have an incredible opportunity to believe in Jesus right now, if you have not already done so.

Then, whenever Jesus will appear for the Rapture to take everyone who believes in him to Heaven, you will be included. Given how terrible the Tribulation will be, the pre-Tribulation Rapture truly is Christians' blessed hope (Titus 2:13).

Please share with your friends, family, and coworkers the good news of what Jesus has done by dying for everyone's sins, so that they can also believe and have eternal life in the New Heaven and New Earth. Also tell them about the Rapture, so that if they do not believe in Jesus before it happens, they might believe in Jesus afterward. Hopefully, if they are warned ahead of time, they will avoid falling for whatever false explanation will be given for the Rapture.

Many Christians also write letters for their loved ones or other people who might be left behind. In such a letter, you can explain in your own words what you believed about Jesus, what the Rapture is, and why you have suddenly disappeared. You can also provide a short summary of what will happen during the Tribulation, and warn people to not take the Mark of the Beast.

Then put copies of your letter in places where they can be found by anyone who enters your home to search for you, or even by people who might break in to find supplies after the Rapture. Perhaps stash a Bible and a copy of this book in a place where you know someone may find it after the Rapture happens.

It is also a good idea for all Christians to find a faithful Bible-believing church to attend. Yet finding a good church is likely to become more difficult as the end times approach.

Regardless of the denomination, as long as the pastor or priest preaches that believing in Jesus is the *only* way to have eternal life, it is probably a decent church.

In contrast, there are some major clues that can generally reveal whether a church has gone astray into false teaching, such as:

1. If the leader teaches that faith in Christ is not enough for anyone to have eternal life because something else must be added, such as good works, water baptism, or speaking in tongues.

The Bible shows these things are unnecessary, because the criminal who believed in Jesus while being crucified next to him never had time for these things. Yet Jesus still promised the criminal that he would be in Heaven with him that same day (Luke 23:39–43).

2. If the leader teaches that the Bible might have errors in it, or that current ideas about morality, psychology, science, or history are superior to the Bible or have made certain parts of the Bible obsolete.

Teaching these things is the same as doubting or denying God's word, which is what led to the first sin (Genesis 3:1–7). A leader who ignores or dismisses parts of God's word risks leading their church into sin.

3. If the leader teaches that God wants to make Christians rich, healthy, and successful in this life, if only Christians would have enough faith or give enough money to the leader's church or ministry.

This is not true, because Jesus said that Christians will still have troubles in this life (John 16:33). Jesus' statement was shown to be true in the lives of the Apostles, such as Paul, who faced many difficult situations (2 Corinthians 11:25–27) and was executed for his faith. Paul's protégé Timothy also had ongoing medical problems, even after he became a Christian (1 Timothy 5:23). God does not make any Christians' lives perfect in this world, but instead, Christians can face difficulties with joy because of the hope we have in Christ (James 1:2–4).

It is very difficult to find a church that you will agree with on every minor topic, or that matches all your personal preferences. However, as long as a church does not fit into one of the above three categories, and the leader preaches that eternal salvation is found *only* by putting your faith in Jesus Christ, it is probably safe to attend.

If finding a faithful church to attend is impossible, you can always pray with and worship God with a small group of other Christians, such as your family or friends. Wherever even as few as two or three Christians gather together, Jesus promises to be there with you (Matthew 18:20). Study the Bible together, and trust that the Holy Spirit will lead you to the truth (John 16:13). Perhaps finding an online pastor to watch who teaches the true gospel of salvation by faith in Jesus Christ alone would also be useful.

Keep on reading your Bible so that you can compare everything you hear at church or from others to what is in Scripture (Acts 17:11). If you do not have a Bible, buy one in a translation that you find easy to read. This author particularly enjoys the Contemporary English Version, the New Living Translation, the New Revised Standard Version, and the English Standard Version.

If you have not read the Bible before, the Book of John is a great place to start. So are the other books of Matthew, Mark, and Luke. The Book of Hebrews is very helpful if you have read the Torah and other parts of the Old Testament, but have not yet read the New Testament. Then work your way through the rest of the New Testament, perhaps prioritizing Acts, Romans, Ephesians, and Galatians, as well as the Book of Revelation, before moving on to the rest of the Bible.

A "study" version of the Bible is sometimes helpful, because these versions provide extra information written by Christian scholars that can help the Bible make more sense. However, it is important to remember that unlike the actual words of the Bible, this extra information is not guaranteed to be correct (2 Timothy 3:16).

Other Christian books may also be helpful to teach you more about Christianity, such as some of the ones that are listed at the end of this book. However, remember that all of these other Christian books (including this book) are just people's opinions and interpretations of the Bible. They can be wrong, but the Bible is completely true. Pray that the Holy Spirit will give you discernment to know what is true and what is false (John 16:13).

If you have the ability, it may also help to stock up on some extra food, bottled water, and basic medicines or emergency supplies. Then, if any local disasters occur between now and the Rapture, you will have something to share with others. Your generosity could save their lives, and even open up the possibility of sharing the gospel with them.

Furthermore, once the Rapture happens, then your supplies will also be a blessing to people who are left behind. Some Christians even store their left-behind letters or small gospel messages called "tracts" in their pantries, so that once these Christians are raptured, left-behind people who are in need of supplies might find these messages and hear the gospel.

In the meantime, keep watching for the signs of the end times, like Jesus instructed. When all the signs begin to happen, then you can be reassured that Jesus' return at the Rapture will happen very soon (Luke 21:25–28).

IF YOU ARE READING THIS AFTER THE RAPTURE

Unfortunately, if you are reading this book after the Rapture has occurred, then the world will be heading into the Tribulation period. Everything that you have read in the above chapters will give you an outline of what to expect, in the order that the events will probably occur.

With the information in this book, you should be able to identify who the Antichrist is, and who the False Prophet is. Now you also know not to believe anything that either of these evil men will say. Especially do not believe the Antichrist when he will say that he is God (2 Thessalonians 2:3–4).

Avoid taking the Mark of the Beast at all costs, and warn others to also not take it (Revelation 14:9–11). Even if you have to die because you refuse to take the

Mark, you can trust that if you have believed in Jesus, you will be resurrected and you will rule with Jesus in his Millennial Kingdom (Revelation 20:4).

Teach what you have learned to others, and warn them not to fall for the coming deception that will be beyond anything the world has ever experienced. This deception will likely be spread through media propaganda, video and audio manipulation technologies, artificial intelligence, extreme censorship and persecution of all dissenting opinions, and more.

The only perfectly-reliable source of truth that you will have is the Bible. God inspired all of Scripture and God does not lie, so the Bible is completely reliable and true (2 Timothy 3:16, 2 Peter 1:21, Titus 1:2, Hebrews 6:18). Therefore, you need to buy or find at least one Bible before they are banned or confiscated.

The homes of people who were raptured will probably have at least one Bible. Check for Bibles on bookshelves, coffee tables, desks, and in bedside tables. Churches and other Christian schools and organizations will also have Bibles in their offices, pews, and libraries. Do not trust any new 'edited' versions of the Bible that may be published by the Antichrist, because they will contain lies. You will likely have to hide your Bible from the authorities if it becomes illegal to own one.

Read the Bible and learn it as fast as you can. The Book of John is a great place to start, and so are the other books of Matthew, Mark, and Luke. The Book of Hebrews is very helpful if you have read the Torah or other parts of the Old Testament, but have not yet read the New Testament. Then work your way through the rest of the New Testament, perhaps prioritizing Acts, Romans, Ephesians, and Galatians, as well as the Book of Revelation, before moving on to the rest of the Bible.

If you are fortunate, there may be other Christian books that you can find that could be helpful. However, remember that all of these other books are just people's opinions and interpretations of the Bible. They can be wrong, but the Bible is completely true. Pray that the Holy Spirit will give you discernment to know what is true and what is false (John 16:13).

You will also need to become absolutely convinced that no matter what someone else tells you, or what supposedly-miraculous signs the Antichrist and False Prophet might perform, you will not stop believing what you know is true about Jesus and the gospel (Galatians 1:8).

The task of holding onto your faith in Jesus will be easier if you can find a supportive group of other people who believe the same things that you now do. Meet together regularly with these other believers to encourage each other, pray for each other, and teach the Bible to each other. Share your resources with each other, like the early church did, and share the truth with whoever else will listen (Acts 2:42–46).

However, be careful about attending any churches that are still operating after the Rapture.

If the leaders of these churches are preaching that the Rapture truly happened, and if they admit that they made a mistake by never truly believing the gospel before the Rapture happened, then that is a good sign that this church may be safe to attend. It is also a good sign if the leaders are warning about the coming Tribulation, and if they are telling people to believe in Jesus in order to have eternal life.

But if you go to a church and the leader is teaching that God, "Gaia," "the universe," or "aliens" removed the "intolerant and hateful troublemakers" and "false believers" from the world, in order for humanity to come together under a single religion and so save the planet and achieve a utopian future of peace, prosperity, tolerance, and "love," then leave that church as fast as you can.

As for how to survive the Tribulation, the Bible does not give much specific advice. The most important thing is to hold onto your faith in Jesus Christ at all costs, which is why the Bible encourages the saints who will live during the Tribulation to have patient endurance (Revelation 13:10, 14:12).

The Bible warns that some Christians will be imprisoned, and others will be martyred (Revelation

13:10). Yet anyone who will be martyred for their faith in Jesus during the Tribulation will be resurrected and rewarded by ruling with Jesus during the Millennial Kingdom (Revelation 20:4).

Unfortunately, the Bible does not offer any advice on how to survive without taking the Mark of the Beast.

It may be wise, if you have the financial ability, to build up a stockpile of long-lasting nutritious food, bottled water or other drinks, basic medicines, and first aid resources. This will be especially important in order to help you survive the Third Seal judgment. It will also enable you to generously help others as a way of sharing God's love with them.

Remember that when you share what you have with others, you are actually sharing with Jesus, who will reward you (Matthew 25:34–40). God can also multiply what you have to make it last far longer than you expect (1 Kings 17:8–16, Matthew 14:13–21).

Yet it is very unlikely that anyone could possibly store up enough supplies in a safe enough location to survive all seven years of the Tribulation. Everyone in the world will be affected—even the multi-millionaires with underground doomsday bunkers and private security guards.

The disasters will be so widespread that many people will need to flee their homes to find safety elsewhere. Many other people will be looting homes and using violence to steal resources from others in order to provide for themselves or their own families. It will be a very dangerous time (Matthew 24:12–13, 2 Timothy 3:1–13).

If you do not have any resources or other people to help you, or if your resources are taken or destroyed, then simply trust that God will somehow provide for you. There are instances recorded in the Bible where God provided food, water, or resources for his faithful people in miraculous ways that they could never have expected (e.g., Exodus 16, 17:1–7, Numbers 11:31–35, 1 Kings 19:5–8).

There are also times when God helped his faithful people miraculously escape from prison when it seemed impossible (Acts 5:17–21, 12:6–11, 16:25–34). Sometimes, God sent dreams to his people to tell them how to avoid danger (Matthew 2:12–19).

If necessary, God can even miraculously override the laws of physics in order to preserve his faithful people's lives. For example, God did this when he kept Daniel's three friends from dying in the fiery furnace when they refused to worship Nebuchadnezzar's idol (Daniel 3:26–28).

Remember that everything will work out for the ultimate good of those who love God (Romans 8:28). This is true regardless of whether you physically survive the Tribulation.

No matter what happens in your future, if you have believed in Jesus as your Savior, you can trust that you will have eternal life in the New Heaven and New Earth (Romans 8:35–39). Then, God will wipe away every tear, and there will be no more suffering ever again (Revelation 21:1–4).

Conclusion

You have now completed an overview of what the Bible says about the end times from a futuristic, pre-Millennial perspective which includes the pre-Tribulation Rapture.

However, due to the complexity of the topic and the unfamiliarity that even many long-time Christians can have with the end times, you may want to read through this book several times, to thoroughly absorb the material, while reading the Bible verses that are referenced in order to examine them in their larger contexts.

If you wish to study the topic of the end times or Christian theology and church history in more detail, a list of some relevant sources is provided at the end of this book.

Not every source will agree with one another or with what is written in this book in every detail. However, if you are familiar with what is written in the Bible, the knowledge that you have gained from reading this book should help you weigh the evidence and arguments that will be made in these other sources.

The Appendix that follows this conclusion discusses a few remaining questions that are still debated among Bible prophecy experts about the Rapture. It also addresses the fate of the United States of America in Bible prophecy, as well as a few major wars between Israel and other nations that are still prophesied to occur in the future, and the relevance of these wars to the end times.

Appendix

Some Remaining Questions

This appendix will address several remaining questions regarding end-times Bible prophecies about which there is more disagreement among Bible prophecy experts.

The answers to these questions are also more difficult to fully support using Scripture, although they can often be seen as logical extensions of what is taught in the Bible.

Therefore, the ideas proposed here are somewhat speculative at points. They are offered here as ideas for the reader to consider, and for the reader to decide whether these interpretations seem plausible.

WILL CHILDREN BE RAPTURED?

A major question about the Rapture is whether children will be raptured.

This question can easily be answered by saying that yes, at least some children will be raptured. This is because at least some children will be Christians at the time of the Rapture, because they will have heard the gospel and personally put their faith in Jesus Christ as their Savior.

Usually, though, what people mean when they ask this question is whether *all* of the world's children could be taken to Heaven in the Rapture, along with Christians.

In particular, people who ask this question often feel a strong concern for children who are not yet old enough to understand the gospel. It seems awful to them to imagine that God would leave behind many children to experience the Tribulation.

Therefore, many prophecy experts argue that when the Rapture happens, all children under a particular age will also be taken to Heaven at the same time.

It is not clear whether these children will also receive immortal bodies at the Rapture, though, like Christians will, or whether these children might be returned to Earth in their mortal bodies after Jesus' Second Coming. In the latter case, these children would finish growing up during the Millennial Kingdom, and so become part of the people who would go on to help repopulate the world during Jesus' Millennial Kingdom.

This theory that all children might be raptured relies on how Jesus showed a special love for children. Jesus said that the Kingdom of Heaven belongs to children (Matthew 19:13–14). He also held up children as models of simple, trusting faith that adults should attempt to copy (Matthew 18:1–4).

However, there are several questions that must be asked. The first question is exactly what is the age limit that could make the difference between a child being raptured and a child being left behind. Will all children under the age of, say, twelve or thirteen be raptured? Or maybe the limit could be even younger? Or will it vary depending on the individual maturity of each child?

In Christian theology, these questions all relate to a concept called the *age of accountability*.

Often, this idea is used by pastors and priests to reassure Christian parents that if their child dies before the child was old enough to personally believe in Jesus, then that child is still going to be with Jesus in Heaven. Yet this idea raises the same questions regarding age limits and personal maturity levels of each child as the question about whether children might be raptured.

There is nowhere in the Bible that specifically or clearly explains when God requires children to become personally responsible for putting their own faith in Jesus Christ as their Savior.

Many arguments are made by well-meaning Christians that claim that children are "innocent," and so they say that children's souls automatically go to Heaven if they die.

There is one verse in the Old Testament that is read as supporting this possibility, when David's son died as an infant because of David's sin with Bathsheba. After his son died, David seemed to have confidence that he would see his son again one day in Heaven (2 Samuel 12:23).

However, all people are born sinners, because they are descendants of Adam and Eve (Romans 5:12–14). Thus, even children need Jesus to have died for their sins, in order for them to have eternal life.

Therefore, more theologically-astute answers to this question tend to get into complicated discussions of how Jesus' death for sin can be applied to children, even without these children having yet expressed personal belief in Jesus. These same answers are often given to support the idea that the souls of people with severe cognitive handicaps who never seemed to have any ability to understand the gospel during their lives will also go to Heaven when they die.

Regarding the Rapture, the most persuasive argument that all children under a particular age and people under a particular level of cognitive ability might also be raptured is to say that God might rapture them to protect them from the evil plans that Satan and his world leaders might have for them. For example, Jesus warned it would be better for anyone who caused children to sin to have a heavy stone tied around their necks, and then be thrown into the sea to drown (Matthew 18:5–6).

Evil will reach its peak on Earth during the Tribulation, and so children would seem to be particularly at risk from Satan, the Antichrist, the False Prophet, and their evil plans for humanity. So the argument is that God might therefore choose to rescue all children by taking them to Heaven, to keep them out of the Antichrist's reach. However, this idea is still difficult to theologically prove.

Depending on how much time there will be between the Rapture and the start of the Tribulation, presumably, more children will be conceived and born on Earth. Jesus even said that some pregnant women and families with young children will be among those in Judea who flee to the mountains after the Abomination of Desolation occurs (Matthew 24:19, Luke 21:23).

It is true that there would be far fewer children on Earth during the Tribulation if most of them under a certain age were raptured. So, if God does choose to rapture all children, it would be an act of God's mercy to save these children from having to die terrible deaths from the judgments that he will bring on the world during the Tribulation.

If all children were raptured, it would also make the Rapture an emotionally-devastating event to the entire world. Otherwise, the Rapture would disproportionately affect only countries with large numbers of Christians.

If all of the world's children were raptured, it may make the people of the world more willing to listen to the Antichrist when he appears. They might quickly accept whatever lie he tells them regarding where their children have gone. The fear caused by a lie that the children were abducted by aliens, for example, might inspire the countries of the world to quickly unite into a world government.

Some pessimists might argue that God will not rapture all children, because many children throughout history have suffered immensely in many different ways, and God did nothing to help them.

Presumably, many children also died during God's other historical judgments such as the worldwide Flood, the destruction of the cities of Sodom and Gomorrah, and the invasions of Jerusalem (e.g., Hosea 13:16). So these pessimists argue that God will leave the children of non-Christian families behind on Earth to suffer through the Tribulation.

However, there is a difference between all previous periods of human history and the Tribulation. The Tribulation will be the absolute worst time in human history (Matthew 24:21–22). It will also be a time when God's own wrath will be directly poured out on the entire world (e.g., Revelation 6:16–17).

In contrast, as terrible as some things were in the past that caused children to suffer or die, these were just the usual troubles and difficulties that a sinful world has faced since the first sin of Adam and Eve (John 16:33).

So there could be a case to be made that God would want to spare as many children as possible from experiencing his own wrath during the Tribulation, even if some additional children will be unfortunate enough to be born during those awful seven years.

On a positive note, these children who will be born after the Rapture would likely remain under God's age of accountability for the entire seven years of the Tribulation. This would probably be true even if there were a gap as long as a few years between when the Rapture happens and when the treaty between the Antichrist, Israel, and "many" is signed, which would officially signal the start of the Tribulation (Daniel 9:27).

So, if any of these young children who were born after the Rapture were to die during the Tribulation, their souls would immediately go to Heaven, provided that the age of accountability theory is true. The remaining children who happen to survive the Tribulation will be lucky enough to grow up during Jesus' Millennial Kingdom.

Therefore, it is not clear whether God will rapture all children. It is also not clear whether God has some specific age range in mind for when he expects children to have their own faith in Jesus, or if it depends on the individual child's personal level of maturity and whether the child has heard the gospel or not.

Yet a more certain answer can be given regarding the children of Christian parents.

Most prophecy experts argue that at least the children of Christian parents will be raptured, if the children are under the age of accountability when the Rapture happens. This would be especially true if the children are so young that they could not survive on their own without parental care.

For example, it is quite easy to believe that a God of perfect love and mercy would not separate a Christian mother from her baby or young child by rapturing her and leaving her helpless child behind. God would also not want raptured Christian parents in Heaven to worry about the fate of their young children left behind on Earth during the Tribulation.

Yet it is more difficult to argue that a teenager would be raptured if he or she had heard the gospel several times at church, Sunday school, or Bible camp, and understood it, but inwardly rejected it. Therefore, there could potentially be some teenagers from Christian families who might be left behind, even if their parents are raptured.

God will wipe away every tear from Christians who mourn the eternal loss of their loved ones after the Final Judgment (Revelation 21:4). By extension, God would surely comfort any Christian parents if they discovered that their teenage child had been left behind after the Rapture. This case would not be much different from Christian parents who would be raptured, but have their unbelieving adult-aged children left behind.

If you are worried about your loved ones being left behind at the Rapture, the best thing to do is to pray for them. Pray that God will open up opportunities for you or others to share the gospel with them. Also pray that they will be willing to listen, and that they will consider putting their faith in Jesus before the Rapture happens.

But if anyone you talk to about these things does not choose to believe in Jesus before the Rapture, there is a very good chance that once the Rapture happens, if they have at least heard about the idea of the Rapture, they will be less likely to believe whatever lie will be told to the world that will claim the Rapture did not happen. Then, these people might also be convinced to believe what they heard about Jesus from Christians who were raptured.

Therefore, these left-behind people would have a high chance of becoming believers in Jesus and being eternally saved after the Rapture. They will face very difficult times and be persecuted for their faith, but that is far better than remaining an unbeliever and facing the second death in the Lake of Fire (Revelation 20:11–15).

Will pets be raptured?

Occasionally, services have been advertised that attempt to make money off of Christians' fears that their pets might be left behind if Christians are raptured. These services might claim that Christians can pay a fee now to sign up to have a certified non-Christian stop by their homes in the case of the Rapture, in order to rescue their pets.

However, the providers of these services seem to underestimate how chaotic the world might become after the Rapture. For example, it may be impossible to drive anywhere for at least several days in many places if roads are blocked with empty cars that need to be towed. Cities might also impose curfews or shelter-in-place orders to deal with the chaos, confusion, and possible looting that will likely occur after the Rapture.

There is also no guarantee that the left-behind people who had signed up to rescue pets will not be more worried about themselves and their own families and friends. It would be easy for them to ignore any promises they made when they thought the Rapture was just a myth, especially if they have already received their payment from Christians.

On the other hand, some notable Bible prophecy experts have taught that the pets of Christians will certainly be taken to Heaven during the Rapture.

They say the reason that Christians' pets will also be taken in the Rapture is because God knows that Christians love their pets. They say that God would not want the raptured Christians in Heaven to worry that their beloved pet was potentially locked inside a home or inside a kennel or cage, and thus be unable to access food or water. This would especially be true if it might take at least several days or weeks for someone to come check on Christians' homes after the Rapture.

God does care for animals, even the smallest of birds (Matthew 6:26). So God would likely have compassion on the pets of raptured Christians, in one way or another.

If Christians' pets are not raptured, God could perhaps ensure that the pets will miraculously escape from their cages or homes. God could also enable left-

-behind family members, friends, or neighbors to find a way to stop by shortly after the Rapture to rescue the pets.

Alternatively, looters might smash windows and pry open doors of Christians' homes in an attempt to find supplies after the Rapture, and the pets could escape that way.

Is the United States of America mentioned anywhere in Bible prophecy?

Many people who are interested in Bible prophecy often wonder about what will happen to the United States of America in the end times.

Because the USA has been so powerful and influential around the world during the last hundred years or so, it seems that the USA should also continue to play an important role during the Tribulation.

Bible prophecy experts usually take one of two different approaches to this topic.

The first approach is to say that the USA will be so devastated by the Rapture that it will lose its position of world influence. This is why it will not be a major end-times player, and this is why the USA is not directly mentioned anywhere in Bible prophecy.

Many demographic studies suggest that currently, about fifty to eighty percent of the USA's adult population claim to be Christian. If this percentage of the population were raptured, along with many or even all children, the USA would surely face a terrible situation. It would probably would lose most of its world influence for at least several years, if not decades, while the minority that were left behind attempt to recover and restructure their society.

However, other studies claim that although a large number of people in the USA claim to be Christian, many of these people may not be true Christians.

These Christians-in-name-only might not believe that salvation depends on having personal faith in Jesus Christ alone. Instead, they might place their trust in their own good works, church attendance, baptism, or what their parents believed. Yet none of these things will save anyone (Ephesians 2:8–9, Romans 11:6).

Some surveys that ask people about their specific religious beliefs show that only about ten percent or less of people in the USA actually have a Biblical worldview. However, because all that matters for salvation is faith in Jesus Christ, there are likely many true Christians who do not have a fully Biblical worldview. Although having a Biblical worldview is very spiritually helpful, no one will be raptured or left-behind on the basis of how Biblical one's worldview was.

So the number of true Christians in the USA is probably somewhere in the range of twenty to forty percent of the entire population. This is still a significant number of people. When the Rapture happens, out of all the countries in the world, the USA will probably be the one that will experience the largest decrease in its population.

Furthermore, if the USA were significantly weakened by the Rapture, it could become a tempting target for its enemies. If the USA were invaded by foreign armies or suffered several devastating nuclear explosions during the Second Seal judgment, it could lose even more influence. This could also explain why the USA is not directly mentioned in Bible prophecy.

However, the second position that Bible prophecy experts sometimes take when discussing the future of the USA is to identify the USA with "Babylon" in Revelation chapters 17 and 18.

This claim is made on the basis of how "Babylon" is described as being extremely wealthy, and as making the merchants of the world wealthy by buying all of their luxury products (Revelation 18:3, 18:11–19).

This seems to be true of the USA today, which buys so many products from around the world that standards of living have rapidly risen in many formerly-poor countries over the last few decades. It is these countries that depend on consumers in the USA and the rest of the Western world to buy their products in order to continue developing their economies.

In the Book of Revelation, despite being symbolized as a prostitute, "Babylon" is also described as being like a "queen" who is full of corruption, immorality, and sin. However, "Babylon" has not experienced major suffering, and it does not seem to expect to face God's judgment for its sins (Revelation 18:7–8).

Some Bible prophecy experts argue that today, America is so full of sin and is such a bringer of immorality and violence to the rest of the world that it is worthy of God's judgment, just like the sinful cities of Sodom and Gomorrah were before God suddenly destroyed them (Genesis 19:1–29). Yet in its history, despite facing some challenges, the USA has not experienced any major setbacks, and it has usually been successful in everything it tried to do.

The identification of "Babylon" as the USA is also possibly supported by how all the kings of the world will have had immoral relations with "Babylon" (Revelation 18:9–10). Today, many countries work to please the USA and keep good relations with it in order to benefit from the USA's military defense or economic trade agreements.

If the USA is symbolically being spoken about in Revelation by using the code name "Babylon," then it seems that God will warn his faithful people to physically get out of the USA, so that they will not suffer from the judgment that it will experience in the last days (Revelation 18:4–6).

This warning would have to be addressed to people who become Christians in the USA after the Rapture, because Christians who live before the Rapture will obviously be raptured before any major disasters will destroy the USA. This claim that the USA will not face destruction or judgment before the Rapture is based on how currently, it is easy to imagine that the world would be thrown into massive upheaval if the USA were to collapse or be destroyed.

The US dollar is widely used for international trade, and the USA is currently the world's greatest military power. Without the USA's financial support, many other countries would fall into poverty or face economic collapse. Many wars would also likely take place around the world because the USA would no longer be able to intervene as readily or reinforce the militaries of the USA's allies.

Yet today, all the other signs of the end times are rapidly increasing in frequency and intensity. Technology is also ready to enable the Mark of the Beast and the Image of the Beast. Therefore, it does not seem like there is enough time for the world to experience such a major upheaval, and then return to a condition of going along normally, before it will be time for the Rapture to occur and the Tribulation to begin (Matthew 24:37–38).

However, a world-changing disaster like the fall of the USA could possibly be what is described in Revelation chapter 18.

In this interpretation, the great "city" of "Babylon" that experiences destruction in a single day and a single hour (Revelation 18:8, 18:17–20) could perhaps refer to the entire USA, or maybe to a major representative city such as New York. This city is currently the center of the USA's financial system. It is also the location of the famous Statue of Liberty monument, which is a significant icon related to the USA that looks like a woman, just as Babylon is symbolically depicted in Revelation as a woman.

It is also the merchants of "Babylon" who are described in the Bible as being the great people of the earth, who have so much power that they can deceive all the nations (Revelation 18:23). Today, many if not most of the world's wealthiest businessmen and most powerful politicians are based in the USA.

Therefore, it seems that many aspects of the Bible's descriptions of "Babylon" could match with the current condition of America. These aspects of "Babylon" also seem to be more accurate descriptions of the USA than of the left-behind remnants of the Roman Catholic Church, which is the more traditional interpretation of "Babylon" that is usually given by Bible prophecy experts.

So it is possible that the Rapture will be much less devastating to the USA than is often expected. Even if as much as ten or twenty percent of the USA's population will be raptured, the USA might be able to recover quickly enough to maintain its position as a world power during the Tribulation.

If "Babylon" does symbolize the USA, then the Book of Revelation could also be implying that the USA will have enough power after the Rapture that it can somewhat control or restrain the Antichrist's global "beast" government during the early parts of the Tribulation (Revelation 17:1–5).

Yet at some point, the Antichrist and his ten world leaders will become tired of being controlled by "Babylon." They will turn on it, plunder its riches, and burn it with fire, all within one day, and even one hour (Revelation 17:16–17, 18:8–10). How this could be done to a country the size of the USA is difficult to imagine.

Therefore, critics of this interpretation prefer the more traditional interpretation that "Babylon" represents a final false world religion. This religion will probably be associated with the corrupt left-behind remnants of the Roman Catholic Church, based on how it is identified with the colors of purple and scarlet, and as having significant wealth (Revelation 17:3–5), as was discussed at various points earlier in this book.

In its own ways, the unbelieving parts of the Roman Catholic Church that will be left behind at the Rapture could also fulfill many of these descriptions of "Babylon." The Roman Catholic Church has also had significant influence over Europe and many other countries around the world. It is very wealthy, and it has also not experienced significant suffering or destruction throughout its history.

The deciding factor as to whether "Babylon" is describing the USA or the left-behind remnants of the Roman Catholic Church may come down to two details:

1. Which one is more closely identified with a single wealthy city that sits on seven mountains that could be destroyed in just one day or hour (Revelation 17:9, 18:16–17, 16:19).
2. Which one has persecuted or will persecute more true Christians throughout history, especially during the early parts of the Tribulation period (Revelation 17:6, 18:24).

Both of these points may fit better with the idea that "Babylon" is a false pseudo-Christian religion based on Roman Catholicism that could rise to power during the beginning of the Tribulation.

If so, then the city that is destroyed by the Antichrist and the ten kings would clearly be Rome, which has the Roman Catholic Church's headquarters at the Vatican within its boundaries. Rome is also geographically located on seven physical hills.

The voice from Heaven that will tell God's faithful people to come out of "Babylon" so that they do not experience its plagues (Revelation 18:4–5) could then be taken as a warning for left-behind people who become Christians after the Rapture to not participate in this false world religion, even if it may initially appear to be a form of ecumenical pseudo-Christianity.

It would then be this false world religion that would turn against and persecute these true Christians who refuse to be part of it. This persecution may begin as early as the Fifth Seal judgment (Revelation 6:9–11).

It is probably true that there will be a large number of people who will be left behind in the USA who believed they were Christians, but actually were not. These people might be easily convinced to join an ecumenical movement based on some form of pseudo-Christianity that could be led by the left-behind Roman Catholic Church. There is a hint that those people who will persecute real Christians during the end times will think they are going God a favor (John 16:2).

So perhaps there could be some connection between the USA and whatever false pseudo-Christian religion might become popular after the Rapture. If so, this could possibly explain the multi-faceted description of "Babylon" found in the Book of Revelation.

However, perhaps it is still currently too early to know for certain what it is that is being called "Babylon" in Revelation chapters 17 and 18.

If "Babylon" does represent the USA in some way, then it seems this is the only portion of Bible prophecy that explains what might happen to the USA during the Tribulation.

If "Babylon" does not represent the USA, then perhaps that is because for one reason or another, the USA will lose its power after the Rapture or during the early judgments of the Tribulation. This could then explain why America is not directly referenced in any clear way in end-times Bible prophecy.

What other Bible prophecies might be fulfilled either before or during the Tribulation?

There are three lesser-known prophecies that many Bible prophecy experts believe will be fulfilled either before or during the Tribulation. However, there is more variation among prophecy experts regarding exactly when these prophecies will be fulfilled.

These prophecies include:

- the Psalm 83 War.
- the Gog-Magog War (Ezekiel 38).

- that Damascus will be turned into a heap of ruins which will never be inhabited again (Isaiah 17).

The Psalm 83 War is not mentioned very often by Bible prophecy experts, and it is the most controversial of the above three prophecies.

It seems to describe an invasion of Israel by certain countries that will form an alliance against Israel. They will want to destroy Israel (Psalm 83:2–4), so that they can claim the land of Israel as their own (Psalm 83:12).

These countries and groups of people are listed using the names that they were known by at the time when Psalm 83 was written (Psalm 83:5–8). These countries included regions that are now in modern-day Jordan (formerly called Edom, Moab, and Ammon), the Gaza Strip (Philistia), Lebanon (Tyre, Gebal, and Phoenicia), Egypt's Sinai Peninsula (Amalek), and Syria (Assyria).

So this Psalm seems to describe an attack on Israel by most of the countries that currently surround it today, which include Jordan, Lebanon, Syria, the Palestinians in Gaza, and parts of Egypt.

This combination of countries has never been recorded as forming an alliance to attack Israel at any point in the past. Therefore, the Psalm 83 war is usually thought to be a future war.

Yet other Bible prophecy experts deny that this is a literal future war that Israel will fight with its neighbors. They say it is only a prayer that God will take vengeance on Israel's enemies in general.

However, the Psalm 83 War seems that it will likely be a real war once the Gog-Magog War is taken into consideration.

In Ezekiel chapter 38, Israel is prophesied as being attacked by another different combination of countries that has never yet occurred. In the original languages, these countries include areas that are now in the modern-day countries of Turkey (formerly called Gomer and Beth-Togarmah), Iran (Persia), Sudan (Cush), and Libya (Put) (Ezekiel 38:3–5).

These countries will be led by a man who is referred to as "Gog," from the land of Magog, who is listed as the chief prince of Rosh, as well as Meshech and Tubal (Ezekiel 38:1–3). In modern-day terms, these regions now include parts of Russia and some of the southern formerly-Soviet Socialist Republics like Kazakhstan, and possibly areas of northern Turkey.

What is interesting about these countries is that, unlike those countries that will be involved in the Psalm 83 War, these countries are not Israel's closest neighbors. Instead, the countries listed in the Gog-Magog War form an outer ring around the countries that are listed as participating in the Psalm 83 War.

The countries in the Gog-Magog War are also said to attack Israel at a time when Israel's people have been regathered back into the land from many different countries, and Israel will be living at peace without needing walls or fences for safety (Ezekiel 38:10–12).

Today, Israel is not living at peace, and there are many fences and checkpoints that separate Israel from its immediate neighbors. However, if Israel's immediate neighbors were defeated in the Psalm 83 War, then Israel might feel safe enough to let its guard down.

It seems the Gog-Magog alliance of countries will attack Israel to try to claim Israel's resources and riches for themselves (Ezekiel 38:10–13). This is interesting, considering that Israel has recently discovered several large natural gas fields just off its coast. Israel is also currently doing well economically, while some other countries in the region are struggling.

Yet the purpose of God in allowing this invasion is to make God's greatness known to the nations of the world. This will occur when God miraculously defeats the Gog-Magog alliance using an earthquake, torrential rain, hail, fire, sulfur, pestilence, and in all this chaos, the soldiers will attack one another (Ezekiel 38:18–23).

When God miraculously protects Israel from this otherwise-overwhelming army, then Israel will recognize that God truly is their God, and the people will turn back to faith in him in large numbers. Other countries will also recognize God as the God of Israel (Ezekiel 39:7–8, 39:21–24).

Therefore, some Bible prophecy experts believe that the Psalm 83 War and Gog-Magog War may take place very early on during the Tribulation, perhaps during the Second Seal judgment.

Alternatively, these two wars could theoretically occur even before the Tribulation begins. God's miraculous protection of Israel could provide Israel with the motivation to agree to the Antichrist's peace treaty or covenant that seems to allow them to rebuild their Temple and re-start their traditional sacrificial system (Daniel 9:27).

Because of all the dead soldiers that will be left in their land, Israel will create a large mass grave in an area that was known to Ezekiel as the Valley of the Travelers (Ezekiel 39:11–13). Once this initial burying is done after seven months, special teams will travel through the land for seven more months to place markers whenever they find human remains, so that any other human remains can be properly buried (Ezekiel 39:14–16).

After this war, the Bible also says that Israel will take all the weapons that were left behind in their land by their deceased enemies and will burn them as fuel, instead of needing to burn their own energy resources (Ezekiel 39:9–10). These weapons will provide Israel with energy for seven years. This is an interesting number, because it is also the same length of time as the Tribulation will last, and could suggest that the two time periods are the same.

However, rather than seeing the Gog-Magog War as being a war that happens at the start of the Tribulation or as a possible precursor to the Antichrist's peace treaty between Israel and "many" (Daniel 9:27), there are some prophecy experts who think the Gog-Magog War is the same as the Battle of Armageddon in Revelation 19.

This could be because the method that God will use to defeat these enemies seems quite similar to what is described at the Battle of Armageddon and the Seventh Bowl judgment (Zechariah 14:12–15, Revelation 16:19–21). The aftermath is also similar, where the dead soldiers' bodies are at least partially eaten by birds (Ezekiel 39:17–20, Revelation 19: 17–21).

However, one difficulty with this interpretation is the contradiction in how the Bible says the Gog-Magog War will be led by the chief prince of Russia (Rosh, Meshech, and Tubal) (Ezekiel 38:1–3). However, the Antichrist will lead the Battle of Armageddon, and his army will involve all of the kings of the world (Revelation 16:12–16), rather than just the few specific countries listed in Ezekiel chapter 38.

Other prophecy experts believe that the Gog-Magog War is the same as the last final rebellion against Jesus that will be instigated by Satan at the end of Jesus' Millennial Kingdom (Revelation 20:7–10). This is because the countries of Gog and Magog are also mentioned as being involved in this final rebellion.

Yet in the Gog-Magog War, God's purpose is to bring Israel back to faith in God, so that they will never again disbelieve in God (Ezekiel 39:22). During the Millennial Kingdom, Israel will be faithful to God, and all people around the world will know God (Jeremiah 31:31–34, Zechariah 14:16–21, Psalm 22:27–31), so there is no need for such a war at the end of Jesus' Millennial Kingdom. Therefore, it seems that the Gog-Magog War must happen sometime before the Millennial Kingdom, which would place it either before or during the Tribulation.

Some prophecy experts also believe that because Ezekiel chapters 38 and 39 describe an army that uses low-tech weaponry such as wooden shields and clubs, spears, bows and arrows, swords, and horses, that it could not be describing a modern war (e.g., Ezekiel 38:4–5, 39:9–10).

In response, those prophecy experts who place the Gog-Magog War at the end of the Tribulation during the Battle of Armageddon suggest that the Antichrist might have to resort to these primitive weapons. If this is true, it might be because all of God's judgments during the Tribulation will have destroyed the world's ability to produce tanks, aircraft, missile launchers, and so forth. Or perhaps a huge solar flare in the Fifth Bowl judgment (Revelation 16:10) will make all of these high-tech weapons useless, as if they had been hit with an electromagnetic pulse attack.

Yet the idea of the Antichrist and the whole world's armies trying to fight against the return of Jesus and his heavenly armies with literal swords and shields creates a rather pitiful image. It would be much more fitting to have the Battle of Armageddon be fought between Jesus' heavenly armies and the Antichrist's armies that are outfitted with all of the modern weaponry that humanity can muster. In this way, it would prove to the world just how invincible and powerful Jesus truly is, since none of the world's best weapons will be able to do anything to him or his heavenly armies.

So perhaps Ezekiel's description of the armies of Gog and Magog as using traditional weapons was just Ezekiel's way of saying that it will be a very strong and well-equipped army, and it should not be seen as specifying the exact types of weapons that will be used.

Therefore, it seems that there are arguments to be made that the Gog-Magog War may not necessarily occur before or during the Tribulation. But other arguments suggest that it could plausibly occur between the Psalm 83 War and when Israel will sign the peace covenant with the Antichrist and "many" in Daniel 9:27.

What may tip the balance in favor of the Gog-Magog War occurring earlier rather than later in Bible prophecy is that currently, Syria has close alliances with Russia and Iran, and Turkey is also an ally of Russia. Therefore, the fact that this Gog-Magog alliance appears to be forming now makes it more likely that the world is seeing the possible set-up for the Gog-Magog War.

If things are now lining up for the Gog-Magog War, then the Psalm 83 War will occur even sooner. Otherwise, it seems that Israel's hostile neighbors would join in with the Gog-Magog countries when they attack Israel. The most plausible reason that they will not do this is because Israel's immediate neighbors' armies will have been defeated earlier during the Psalm 83 War.

This brings up one final prophecy that may be fulfilled either before or during the Tribulation, or perhaps during the Psalm 83 War itself. It is the destruction of the city of Damascus, as prophesied in Isaiah chapter 17.

As is the case for all of these prophecies, Damascus has never yet been destroyed so that it became an uninhabitable heap of ruins where only animals live (Isaiah 17:1–2). It also seems that Israel will suffer in some ways by losing crops, and some of its cities will become deserted (Isaiah 17:3–9).

Many Bible prophecy experts believe that this might describe some sort of attack on Damascus using a nuclear weapon, which occurs overnight (Isaiah 17:14). Such an attack may leave Damascus suffering from nuclear fallout, which is why the surviving people would evacuate, and only animals would live there. A nuclear explosion could also explain why some regions in northern Israel near Syria might also be negatively affected.

Yet it is not clear when this attack on Damascus occurs in relation to the Psalm 83 War, the Gog-Magog War, or the signing of the peace treaty between Israel and the Antichrist that begins the Tribulation. It seems that the destruction of Damascus could possibly occur during Psalm 83, because Syria is mentioned as an enemy of Israel in that war, but not in the Gog-Magog War

If Israel were to use a nuclear weapon against Damascus during the Psalm 83 War (or even if Israel were falsely accused of doing so), it could perhaps provide an additional reason that the Gog-Magog alliance would want to attack Israel.

However, there are multiple ways that all of these different prophecies could be fulfilled either before or during the Tribulation.

This author believes that the most likely combination is for Psalm 83 to occur before the Tribulation, which may coincide with the Isaiah 17 destruction of Damascus. Then the Gog-Magog War could occur sometime after this, such as during the Second Seal judgment early on in the Tribulation.

The Psalm 83 War could occur before the Rapture, but it might also occur shortly after. If the United States will be temporarily disabled by the chaos of the Rapture, Israel's nearby enemies might take it as a prime opportunity to try to destroy Israel when the USA could not come to Israel's defense, thus leading to the Psalm 83 War.

One or more of these incidents could also be the reason the Antichrist would sign a peace treaty between Israel and many others (Daniel 9:27). Then the world will say there is peace and security, before it faces sudden destruction during the onset of the Tribulation (1 Thessalonians 5:3).

Recommended Sources For Further Study

Listed below are a selection of books that have contributed to this author's worldview and understanding of Christianity, the gospel, Church history, and the end times as they were put forth in this book.

Alcorn, Randy. *Heaven.* Carol Stream, IL: Tyndale House Publishers, 2004.

Bates, Gary. *Alien Intrusion: UFOs and the Evolution Connection.* Updated and Expanded. Powder Springs, GA: Creation Book Publishers, 2004.

Beale, G. K. *The Book of Revelation.* The New International Greek Testament Commentary. Grand Rapids, MI: Wm. B. Eerdmans Publishing Co., 1999.

Beale, G.K. *The Use of Daniel in Jewish Apocalyptic Literature and in the Revelation of St. John.* Lanham, MD: University Press of America, 1984.

Bing, Charles C. *Simply By Grace: An Introduction To God's Life-Changing Gift.* Grand Rapids, MI: Kregel Publications, 2009.

Boyd, Gregory A. and Paul Rhodes Eddy. *Lord or Legend? Wrestling With The Jesus Dilemma.* Grand Rapids, MI: Baker Books, 2007.

Cook, Stephen L. *The Apocalyptic Literature.* Interpreting Biblical Texts Series. Nashville, TN: Abingdon Press, 2003.

Gregg, Steve. *Revelation: Four Views.* Nashville, TN: Thomas Nelson Publishers, 1997.

Gonzalez, Justo L. *The Story of Christianity.* 2 Vols., Revised and Updated. New York, NY: HarperCollins, 2010.

Hodges, Zane C. and Robert N. Wilkin. *Tough Texts: Did Jesus Teach Salvation By Works?* Denton, TX: Grace Evangelical Society, 2017.

Hitchcock, Mark. *Who Is The Antichrist?* Eugene, OR: Harvest House Publishers, 2011.

Howe, Thomas A. *Daniel In The Preterists' Den: A Critical Look At Preterist Interpretations of Daniel*. Eugene, OR: Wipf and Stock, 2008.

Jeffrey, Grant R. *Apocalypse: The Coming Judgment of the Nations*. New York, NY: Random House, 1994.

Jeffrey, Grant R. *Countdown To The Apocalypse*. Colorado Springs, CO: Waterbrook Press, 2008.

Lahaye, Tim. *Revelation Unveiled*. Grand Rapids, MI: Zondervan, 1999.

McDowell, Josh and Sean McDowell. *Evidence For The Resurrection*. Ventura, CA: Gospel Light, 2009.

Mounce, William D. *Mounce's Complete Expository Dictionary of Old & New Testament Words*. Grand Rapids, MI: Zondervan, 2006.

Madueme, Hans and Michael Reeves, eds. *Adam, the Fall, and Original Sin: Theological, Biblical, and Scientific Perspectives*. Grand Rapids, MI: Baker Academic, 2014.

Nadler, Sam. *The Messiah in the Feasts of Israel*. Revised Edition. Charlotte, NC: Word of Messiah Ministries, 2010.

Olson, Roger E. *The Mosaic of Christian Belief*. Second Edition. Downers Grove, IL: IVP Academic, 2016.

Olson, Roger E. *The Story of Christian Theology*. Downers Grove, IL: IVP Academic, 1999.

Osborne, Grant R. *Revelation*. Baker Exegetical Commentary on the New Testament. Grand Rapids, MI: Baker Academic, 2002.

Ryrie, Charles C. *Dispensationalism*. Revised and Expanded. Chicago, IL: Moody Publishers, 2007.

Walvoord, John F. *Daniel*. The John Walvoord Prophecy Commentaries. Edited by Charles H. Dyer and Philip E. Rawley. Chicago, IL: Moody Publishers, 2012.

Walvoord, John F. *Every Prophecy of the Bible*. Colorado Springs, CO: David C. Cook, 2011.

Walvoord, John F. *The Millennial Kingdom*. Grand Rapids, MI: Zondervan, 1959.

Walvoord, John F. *The Rapture Question*. Revised and Enlarged Edition. Grand Rapids, MI: Zondervan, 1979.

Walvoord, John F. *Revelation*. The John Walvoord Prophecy Commentaries. Edited by Philip E.

Rawley and Mark Hitchcock. Chicago, IL: Moody Publishers, 2011.

Wilkin, Robert N. *The Grace New Testament Commentary.* 2 Vols. Denton, TX: Grace Evangelical Society, 2010.

Other Books By Arden Kierce

Heresies About Jesus Christ: A Short Historical Overview

https://www.amazon.com/dp/B09NQTYM88/

Printed in Great Britain
by Amazon